hey! love them and they will come!

hey! love them and they will come!

V. Bailey Gillespie
Timothy J. Gillespie

Hancock Center Publications
Academic and Professional Books
La Sierra University, Riverside, California
and Advent*Source*, Lincoln, Nebraska

To Hannah Jane
Jacob Owen
Isaac Seth
Bailey Jessica
Emma Grace

*and everyone's children and grandchildren
who make the future of God's Kingdom
so very real and important*

contents

acknowledgments

After almost forty years of involvement in the lives and challenges of young people and their faith growth, surviving nurturing two wonderful and exceptional children—much of that time in parenting —youth work and teaching, I need a very long list of people who have helped my understanding of youth and young people in church- and school-based youth ministry. But even with that disclaimer, I want to identify a few people that have made a significant difference in my ministry and who must be mentioned.

The co-author of this book, Timothy Gillespie, my son, is by far the best colleague I could ever have in ministry. His work with young people in both local congregations, as former chaplain of one of the largest Seventh-day Adventist high schools in its system and at this writing, young adult [RE:Live] pastor at a large university campus, makes his expertise in practical application of good theology and theory an easy choice to share concerns about involving youth and young adults in local congregations. Without his clear thinking, suggestions, and practical consultation, this book could not have been completed. Kudos to him for taking the time to collaborate on this volume and for giving me the chance to articulate clearly the basics of ministry and the reasons why we do what we must do.

There is no way to thank the system that supports publications of this kind, but the North American Division of Seventh-day Adventists provides continued assistance to the John Hancock Center for Youth and Family Ministry at the School of Religion at La Sierra University through assignments that help to illustrate the goals of our ministry and focus us on the multiple age groups within the church. So in a general way, we want to thank them and let the church know we value the opportunity to share what we've learned and what we hope will happen to continue to support change and growth in local congregations.

In this regard the Ministerial Department of the North American Division early on recognized the need to translate the results of our research on young people into a practical guide for local pastors and church leaders. Dave Osborne, a pastor of a large California church and former director of the ministerial department of the North American Division of Seventh-day Adventists, provided both financial support and encouragement to this project. Recognizing need is a wonderful quality. Thanks.

We also thank two other groups. The many volunteer adult youth and young people's leaders with whom we have shared the concepts of this book and the professional youth leaders who share our vision of a youth-focused and inclusive church that sees the value of the young in the sharing of the good news of God's rich grace. And in addition, the youth and young people who make up the masses of young in churches throughout the world cannot be forgotten either. We salute you. We appreciate you. And we challenge you to both have patience with your church and to keep the centrality of a Christ-filled life right in the center of your focus. We feel confident that we can turn this church over to your competent hands and we'll see the growth and commitment increase among your own children as time goes on.

V. Bailey Gillespie, Ph.D.
Timothy J. Gillespie, D.Min.
April, 2011

before you begin

There is a confession in Doug Field's book, *Your First Two Years in Youth Ministry* where he shares this sentence about his challenge. He says, "This book is very different from most other youth ministry books you've seen. It's not a how-to manual—it's a heart-to-heart talk. It's story sharing. It's truth telling." We feel the same way. Good ministry is only done when we are realistic: realistic about our goals and our motives; realistic about our perceptions of what God wants us to do; realistic about our young people; and even more important, realistic about the church that nurtures them.[1]

become a good observer

This close look at the young and their local church means that we will have to be good observers. And good observation means that we are honest about what we see. If we criticize the church, we do so based on loyalty and a desire for change. And any criticism must be viewed as an observation based on research and as a clear opportunity to do it better next time. The past twenty years of research has shown us that people change and, often sadly, people don't change. Churches change and still they, too, don't change. And in order to be helpful and useful we need to deal directly with the problems we've seen and try to suggest ways to correct them . This is especially true for those that hinder faith growth and commitment and loyalty to the church.

Hey! Love them and they will come! is an attempt for a father and son to talk together about what worked in our lives and what we have seen work in the lives of those we've served through ministry. Much of what we've learned has come from research, but another part of this book comes from what we've observed. I have taught for almost forty years, everything from eighth grade through high school, college, university, and graduate and professional school. And most of the time during this process of instruction, I've tried to be both a teacher and learner. On the other side of the coin, Timothy has been a recipient of ministry and parenting. Some of it was helpful; more, perhaps, was not, but all-in-all, we did our best trying to explain and demonstrate to him what religious life is all about. His day-to-day observations into the lives and change of the youth he nurtures gives him an immediate relevance. This is something everyone benefits from and all need.

Timothy's contribution to this book is invaluable in that he is working on a day-to-day basis programming, applying, sharing, and illustrating God's grace to young people. He's corrected and challenged me to be practical and true to what we know about faith development.

We want to be true to what we know about how people learn. For example, young people learn via a number of approaches.

() By interaction and observation.

() By making choices through logical, cognitive development.

() Through experience itself.

() Through indirectly the lives of important peers and adults.[2]

We'll try to provide the theory built on sound theology and applied with creative insights in order to make this book as useful and helpful as possible.

our target audience

Pastor, this book is for you. It was written with the local church in mind. Someone once said to me, "If you don't have the pastors on board, it just won't happen!" If this is true, then you're our first target. But most ministry for children and youth is coordinated by volunteers, so you, lay leader, are another individual who we hope will read this book. After all, you are in the trenches every week. It is you who must teach that Bible lesson at 9:30 - 10:30 a.m. one day each week, month after month. Just doing it right is our goal. Helping you do it well is our target. We want you to use this book to get ideas and methods that have worked and just might make a difference as you mentor your young people.

We can't leave out parents either. While this book is for the church, the church spins off the home in concentric circles. What happens in the home is often reflected in the attitude young people have for their church. So parents can't be left out. The most powerful influence in the faith development of your children is the quality of early family life. Use the ideas presented here to form your worships, create activities for your family, and help you get involved with your own children. After all, what better way to understand the youth of the church than to lead your own children to the Kingdom of God's grace and help them love the church that holds your attention.

Local youth and young adult leaders and religious education professionals can grow as well with reflection of this content.

how to use this book

We target commitment. We hope you accept to the challenge of involving young people in the life and ministry of your local congregation. But to do so takes commitment—real focused, determined commitment. You have to commit to serve the young people of your church and to commit to loving young people. You may have to reallocate your time. After all, if they are important, they deserve your utmost time commitment. You may need to become a learner. Some of the challenges we'll point out may require you to rethink your priorities. Making change is always threatening, but if the goal is to help young people become active in the local church, then the church must be the sole motivator of that change. So make some new commitments right here before we begin. And as Doug Fields again suggests,[3] move slowly and heed the Old Testament counsel in Proverbs 14:15-16. *"A simple man believes anything but a prudent man gives thought to his steps. A wise man fears the Lord and shuns evil, but a fool is hotheaded and reckless."* Think through what we suggest and see if it could be applied to your local congregation. You know your church, and if the needs we've identified apply to you, then, carefully, prayerfully, try to implement the change that may get your youth involved in the church, your family, in the life of God.

There is so much to do, and as the time continues to be shortened because of the era in which we live, we want to make careful use of ideas that will grow the Kingdom of God. Pastors, parents, and adult leaders and volunteers who make church happen each week are key to making this difference. It is this difference we seek. Different attitudes. Different priorities. Different responses. Different choices. It is commitment to the centrality of Jesus in youth's lives that brings a difference. It is the ONE difference because He is the ONE person that made a difference.

Use this book for discussion and ideas. Give the *"Try this"* a chance and see if getting involved in the lives of the young in your congregation helps them see how the church can help them in their growth in grace. The reason this is crucial is because we have so few ways to see how God touches real lives. The church, as God's agency on earth, is one means where the nature of God is demonstrated and the personality of Christians reflects the nature of God. Wouldn't it be a shame if we didn't try everything we could to represent God clearly in a world that is challenging, dangerous, and above all else, the recipient of God's loving gifts?

before you begin / endnotes

1. Doug Fields, *Your First Two Years in Youth Ministry* (Grand Rapids, MI: Zondervan, 2002), 15.
2. See John M. Dettoni, *Introduction to Youth Ministry* (Grand Rapids, MI: Zondervan, 1993) for a complete look at the classic ways youth learn about God.

chapter 1

try loving them

There are so many reasons why this book is important for your church that we don't know exactly where to begin. But for starters, let's just say without young people in your church, you don't really have a church!

Remember what the New Testament suggests. Your church is like a well-functioning human body. It is composed of hundreds of parts, every part working together to make the whole function without disease or problems. Together, there is potential for accomplishment. Apart, there is disaster.

The church is a lot like that. Everyone has a place, everyone has a function, everyone is important if, and I want to emphasize the "if," everything works together. So that is why we wrote this book—to get us to think about how important everyone is in the church, and to target an often neglected population in our community of faith. Your youth and young people.

why this book is important

The youth and young adults in your church all too often feel left out, ignored, and sense that they are not crucial to its purpose and mission. We want to expel this myth and debunk it right here and now. And this book has as its primary goal this purpose—to not only show and share with you why youth and young adults are crucial for your church to truly be church, but to give you some creative, real, and relevant ideas as to how you can involve youth in the life and ministry of your congregation.

A few years back there was a movie about a baseball field that a farmer built in his corn field. Everyone thought he was crazy because he didn't have a baseball team, stands, or league, but he had a dream that if he built it, they would all come. And, in this story, they did. In many ways this is a truism that can apply to our ministry with youth and young adults in our local churches. But to prove my point we have to share some of the research that the Hancock Center for Youth and Family Ministry at La Sierra University and the North American Division Office of Education has completed.

It's called *Valuegenesis* research and it has to do with how you build faith, values, and commitment in homes, schools, and churches. So before we begin, we want to share with you some important research findings that guide the philosophy and theory behind this book.

Now, if you don't like statistics, don't be afraid. This book is trying to be practical, not theoretical, and the data we are going to share is only here because it has relevance to our practice of ministry. The big word that describes this activity is "praxis." It is our praxis that defines what we do. So let's get started on this journey; it is a journey that is filled with excitement, creative ideas, and practical suggestions.

All along the way we'll drop in the facts that support what we believe should be done in ministry to the youth and young in your church using the latest *Valuegenesis* research and trying not to forget to share common sense suggestions.

what is valuegenesis research?

It all began in 1990 when the North American Division of Seventh-day Adventists, Office of Education began to review the educational system of the church. There were concerns about how to build quality in our schools, how to finance the rising tuition costs, what to do about marketing Christian private education, and how faith, values and commitment grow. The last concern spawned the research called *Valuegenesis*—a study of growing maturity of faith and internalizing of values in the lives of the young in the church. We surveyed over 13,000 young people.

We repeated the research ten years later. And with over 20,000 respondents to our surveys, we realized that a lot had changed. And in future books we will update this research with our 2010 analysis. In all our research, however, the three venues—home, church, and school—provide the best opportunities to make a real difference in the spiritual lives of our young people. Whether they were in Adventist educational situations or in the public sphere, the home and the church especially made an important difference. And to make a long research report shorter, we want to focus solely on the local church as an important place where faith is nurtured. We discovered that there are some things that you can do in the church to help faith mature. And conversely, things you should avoid if you don't want the possibility of mature faith to diminish. So that's what drives this book. The suggestions we make here come from that body of work stretching over ten years.[1] We believe that the more we can do to minister—really minister—to the young in the church, the better is the chance that those young people will choose a life of faith and involvement over time in their local church.

ten things we know for sure

Let's begin with what we know works. We won't hide these inside later chapters only to have them jump out at you some time from now! Let's begin by asking two important questions:

◊ So now what makes a real difference in the religious lives of the young people in our local churches?

◊ What can we do to insure their involvement in the church?

We want you to know ten important things that make a difference. Once we clarify these, we can move to the creative section of the book and begin to make sure our praxis is consistent with our theology and theory. So here they are and you can begin to implement these right now, too.

1. The title of the books says it all. "Love them and they will come." Start right now and take the temperature of your church. On a scale of one to five, how would you rate your church in this area. Does your church love the young people that attend? What is the general climate at your church? One of the most important things we have learned is that a warm, open, and supportive climate in local churches makes all the difference. If the young feel accepted and loved, they will feel that there is a place for them in their church. In fact, much is correlated with warm climate in the local church. Do you want to help nurture a rich, and growing faith life? Spend time making sure that the young people in your church feel accepted and know that their church membership loves and includes them. And by "include" we mean that there is an active attempt, a planned approach, an intentional ministry in the church to change the climate.

Now, how can you tell what your climate is like? What can you do to check this out?

try this. *Climate Survey.* You'll need a clipboard and copies of the following survey questions. Ask your youth to talk to adults after the worship service next Sabbath. Compile their answers and see what kind of a score you get. (On a scale of 1 to 5 with 5 being the highest score [yes] and 1 being the lowest [no], how do you rate your answers on the following questions? You can select any score between 1 and 5)

1-2-3-4-5 Q. 1. Our church is a friendly church.
1-2-3-4-5 Q. 2. Do you think strangers usually feel welcome?
1-2-3-4-5 Q. 3. Our church is known for its warmth to visitors
1-2-3-4-5 Q. 4. Our church is open to new ideas.
1-2-3-4-5 Q. 5. Our church includes young people in its decisions.
1-2-3-4-5 Q. 6. I know who the local youth leaders are.
1-2-3-4-5 Q. 7. Do you know my name?
1-2-3-4-5 Q. 8. Does our church have regular teen ministry?
1-2-3-4-5 Q. 9. Do we have a pathfinder club?
1-2-3-4-5 Q. 10. Do you know what our youth budget is?

Each person can count their scores and use a percentage score total. Take your total and double it; that will be your percentage score. (Grade your totals for your church. 90% or above = A; 80% or above = B; 70% or above = C; 60% or above = D; 50% or less = F). Give your church a total report card grade.

2. Help your adult volunteers be dynamic and excited about their own experience with Jesus. It's not the flashy brochures and posters that make a good ministry happen. And contrary to some youth ministry philosophies, mature faith does not come by memorizing a list of twenty-seven beliefs or graduating from a baptismal class. Remember, faith life is not a set of beliefs, it is a process. It is about life change and transformation, not mastery of a set of doctrinal statements. Deep understanding and commitment to doctrines comes best after we are motivated to learn and dig deeper.

Since young people live their lives in the midst of action and choices, the people that nurture this new-found faith have to be people of integrity, commitment and dynamism. The significant word that comes to mind in this group is the word "dynamic." It comes from a Greek root linguistically and it is the foundation for our word "dynamite." People change and accept values when they are impacted by the presence of dynamic people, Christians who are enthusiastic about their faith, their love for Jesus, and their ministry. People who have a sense of the importance of the decisions of life and want to see young people make choices that will impact their future in a positive way. So if you want your young people involved in the church, plan now to select leaders and adult volunteers that are excited about their own faith experience and are comfortable sharing that excitement 24/7.

This implies planning. Don't ever let people become young people's leaders or children's ministry personnel who do so because they just want to get involved. Hand pick your leaders long before you need them to begin. Train them, equip them, and make sure they are excited about the young people they serve. Involvement happens best when those that lead are truly dynamic in their leadership.

You all remember someone in your life that influenced you. Perhaps it was a teacher, pastor, friend of the family, or relative. The impression they made in your life continues to this day. You can be the one that helps others too. So go on, get dynamic about your religious life and share that excitement with those you serve.

try this. *Bible Text Shout.* Volunteer your young people for the scripture lesson in your church service in about two weeks. Print out a passage that is filled with images and excitement. (See Psalm 96). Type up the passage with every other verse assigned to a different group of young people. Have them deliver this reading with real excitement. *(Some of the lines should be shouted, others whispered, some with various words emphasized).* You will have to show them how to do it, I am sure. So let your own involvement show. It's your chance to help them raise their voices in praise.

Practice. Practice. Practice. Do so until the children or youth know the passage and can get totally involved with the praise to God that the passage shares. Show the church everyone is involved in sharing this Psalm of praise. Your involvement will encourage their participation and your excitement about this passage will be contagious.

3. Make the environments user friendly. Another powerful aspect of local churches is the environment where religious education and worship occur. Environment is so crucial, we often change our behavior simply because of the type of environment we happen to be in. You don't go to the bank dressed in a bikini, and you just don't visit an expensive department store in motorcycle leathers and helmet. In the same way, the way the room looks, the way the church represents God, the art used to decorate each grade-level room is important. Environment does make a difference.

Remember when you went camping last? When the sun went down over the horizon and the soft pastel shades of the evening began to creep across the landscape? How did it make you feel? That environment did have an impact on your behavior. Therefore, make the religious places we visit ooze God's presence, love, and power.

Here's a check list for your church young people's leaders. If you want your young people involved, see how high they score. If they score between 80 and 100, then your church is user friendly and has created an environment that is sure to point to God and help the young people of your congregation to keep their minds toward God. If you are a pastor and want to take this yourself, just change the wording to talk about you.

try this. *Church-Friendly Environment.* Give yourself 10 points for every correct answer. If your total is above 80 then you're well on your way to a user friendly church for the young people in your congregation.

"Give yourself 10 points if you. . ."

_____ 1. Have posters on the walls of your church room that reflect a contemporary situation or issue young people face.

_____ 2. Have involved the young people of your church in the design and painting of your church room.

_____ 3. Have a list of all of the young people which includes their birth dates, siblings, and grade in school.

_____ 4. Have invited older young people to mentor your church class.

_____ 5. Have enough adult help to provide one leader or assistant

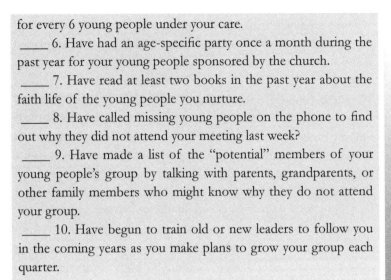

for every 6 young people under your care.

_____ 6. Have had an age-specific party once a month during the past year for your young people sponsored by the church.

_____ 7. Have read at least two books in the past year about the faith life of the young people you nurture.

_____ 8. Have called missing young people on the phone to find out why they did not attend your meeting last week?

_____ 9. Have made a list of the "potential" members of your young people's group by talking with parents, grandparents, or other family members who might know why they do not attend your group.

_____ 10. Have begun to train old or new leaders to follow you in the coming years as you make plans to grow your group each quarter.

4. Be relevant. Research regularly reinforces the fact that relevancy is the best way to increase commitment and loyalty. Relevancy means being real! Are the topics you choose to talk about the ones that your young people are talking about? Do you know the latest hot songs and groups? Can you talk about the sport teams that have been winning and do you know the latest fads that your young people are being influenced by as they go to school? And on a more serious note, do you know the issues your young people are facing regarding their parents, challenges, school problems, and family issues? Do you know the faith development issues the age you work with finds important? If not, then you have some homework ahead.

Being relevant is not easy. It takes some work. Listen to MTV for 20 minutes a day as a start. After all, many of the youth in your church spend more time than that watching TV or playing video games. Learning to be relevant is a challenge: it stretches you beyond what is comfortable; it teaches you to listen.

All too often we don't hear what is bothering the youth in our church. And it is really difficult to predict just how any given adolescent will react to his or her problems. There are a lot of things that impact this reality. Personality traits and environmental factors often impact an adolescent's coping mechanisms. But as you learn to listen to young people, really hear what is important to them, what's real, so to speak, we come to realize that there are only a few ways that they work through their problems, and a caring adult who truly listens can be a tremendous help in keeping these youth near to the church and to provide help in problem-solving.

Many young people cope with their challenges and problems by keeping them to themselves. When they do this, they often sublimate or transform their behaviors into more acceptable ones. Listening carefully can help you to determine what is bothering the young person. Perhaps they are angry at their parents, or their disguised hostility spills over in involvement in sports or music. Or another way their struggles are hidden is to watch them insolate themselves from others to keep the pain away. And some youth even rationalize the struggles away by using their logical skills. Still others act out in ways that are upsetting to adults, while all the time the real reason for the problems they are having are really about something else in their lives.

What's best, however, is to help the young work through their problems, and this takes a helping hand, a caring adult, an understanding peer, or a caring church. So remember to listen, be relevant, keep up-to-date, and recognize what's really driving the interest or disinterest in your youth's lives.

try this. *An exercise in active listening.*[2] Important feelings are often hidden behind the words of a struggling adolescent. Reflecting an adolescent's feelings is one of the most helpful and difficult listening techniques to implement. Following are some typical adolescent statements. Read each separately, listening for feelings. Make note of the feeling you hear and write a response that reflects the feeling of each statement. *(Note that something else is going on behind the simple statement).*

1. I practice all the time, but it doesn't make any difference.
2. Every girl has a date but me.
3. I shouldn't have slammed the door, but she shouldn't have said that.
4. I should be able to stay out past midnight like all of my friends.
5. Do you think I did the right thing?
6. I'd like to punch his lights out!
7. I don't want to talk about it anymore.

8. What's the use?

9. What if she laughs at me? I'm not going to talk to her again.

10. I don't feel anything about it.

11. I don't believe that anymore.

How do you rate in recognizing adolescents' feelings? Go to footnote #3 at the end of this chapter and check possible answers. Give yourself one of the ratings below:

Above average recognition of feelings

Average recognition of feelings

Below average recognition of feelings[3]

It has been said, "God gave us two ears and one mouth—figure it out!"[4] If you're going to be a good shepherd to the sheep, you have to know where they're going on their journey. Periodically take the time to get with young people just to talk. You'll learn an enormous amount just listening and hearing them interact.

5. Young people have something to offer your church. If you want your young people involved in the local church, it is important to recognize the natural gifts that God has given the young which can benefit the local congregation. All too often we think the other way around. We say, "What does the church have to offer the youth?" While this question is important, it is not the first one to ask. Rather, what is it that you can offer the church? Let's start here. What is the obvious answer?

Young people have *time* and *energy*. They are in school, but don't usually work full-time. They have regular hours, so it is easier to program around these regular schedules. You don't have to worry about getting out the youth to a luncheon; they simply are never available at that time. But this time issue does pose challenges. For example, youth have after-school sports and music events and practice. This means after-school programming is difficult at best.

Another factor regarding time is that young people are at the mercy of adults who must drive them, bus them, or drop them off at the church. Older youth, a minority who have cars, have to have parents' permission in order to become fully involved. So you have a dual communication challenge. Both preteens and teens have to be linked to their parents, and they must be equally informed as to the programs and ministry of the local church.

Does your church have a regular means of communication to both families and young people? If not, think how you might accomplish keen communication and at the same time notify parents of the need for their youth to be involved. Bulletin announcements just are not enough. Theory suggests you must contact people at least nine times in order for anyone to remember what's happening!

Now, what about their energy? The young have what seems to be an endless supply. Your church can capitalize on this character quality. Here is a short list of places where the energy of the young in your church can be a blessing.

() Don't do a walkathon, have a work-a-thon and clean up the church campus.

() Need brochures shared with neighbors near your church inviting them to be a visitor? Youth have the time and ability to share their knowledge of their own home church with those nearby.

() Every church needs a community service day where they simply volunteer to help people in need. Organize the youth group and match each with an adult partner and go to work.

() Put your young people on a volunteer team in your church to do whatever is needed.

() Need help? Have your youth enlist adult volunteers for a project they need to do.

() Don't have enough children's teachers? Take one day a month and enlist the help of five to seven young people. Give them the information ahead of time and even go over their teaching assignment. They will do a great job.

() Talk to the youth and if you see ministerial potential, share your observations. Ministry takes root early on in many people, and it provides a valuable option for a vocational choice when they go on to higher education.

You can run on and on with ideas about using the gift of energy in your church. But all too often young people are under utilized in congregational life. But above all, remember that the young have much to offer your church family. The power of involvement in learning about God's kingdom can't be underestimated. *The rule is that everyone learns best through involvement.* When we experience something we retain approximately 80% of the content as opposed to only 5-10% of what we hear. So begin to use the gifts of the young.

try this. *Make a Gift List.* At the first of a new quarter or year, place a large scroll of paper on a table in the front of the church. Ask everyone in the church, younger and older, to write down their name and what gift they think they have. Before you do this, preach a sermon or give a worship talk about the gifts of the Holy Spirit. Identity them. Then sort the gifts and begin to use them in the church. Don't forget to include everyone of all ages.

Here is a list of gifts of the spirit you can use to begin.[5]

() *Administration.* The gift that enables a believer to formulate, direct, and carry out plans necessary to fulfill a purpose. (1 Corinthians 12:28, Acts 14:23).

() *Artistry.* A gift that gives the young person the skill of creating artistic expressions that produce a spiritual response of strength and inspiration. (Exodus 31:1-11, Psalm 149:3).

() *Craftsmanship.* A gift that makes the young person aware of his or her ability to create, build, maintain or repair items. It is a gift that is widely needed in the church today. Used within the church. (Exodus 30:1-6, Exodus 31:3-5, Ezekiel 27:4-11).

() *Discernment.* This gift motivates a young person to seek God's will and purpose and apply that understanding to personal and local congregational issues. (John 16:6-15, Romans 9:1, 1 Corinthians 2:9-16).

() *Evangelism.* The gift that moves young people to reach nonbelievers in such a way that they are moved from just being one of the crowd to become core members of the Christian community. (Matthew 28:16-20, Ephesians 4:11- 16, Acts 2:36-40).

() *Exhortation.* This is a big word that simply moves the young person to reach out with love and presence to people in personal conflict and in need of spiritual help. (John 14:1, 2 Timothy 1:16-18, 3 John 5-8).

() *Faith.* A gift that gives a young person the eyes to see the Spirit at work and the ability to trust God's leading without knowing where it all might lead. (Genesis 12:1-4a, Mark 5:25-34, I Thessalonians 1:8-10).

() *Giving.* This gift that enables one to recognize God's blessings and to respond to them by generously and sacrificially giving of one's resources (time, talent, and treasure). (2 Corinthians 9:6-15, Luke 21:1-4).

() *Hospitality.* A word we don't often use that refers to the gift that causes a believer to joyfully welcome and receive guests and those in need of physical help (Food, lodging, homes, church, etc.). (Romans 12:13, Romans 16:23a, Luke 10:38).

() *Intercession.* The gift that provides power to a believer to pray with certainty. (Matthew 6:6-15, Luke 11:1-10, Ephesians 6:18).

() *Knowledge.* One gift that drives a young person to learn, analyze and uncover new insights with regard to the Bible and faith. (I Corinthians

12:8; I Corinthians 14:6, Romans 12:2).

() *Leadership.* The gift that gives a believer the confidence to step forward, give direction and provide motivation to fulfill a dream or complete a task. (Romans 12:8, John 21:15-17, 2 Timothy 4:1-5).

() *Mercy.* This gift motivates a young person to have empathy for those in need and then act to help. (Luke 7:12-15, Luke 10:30-37, Matthew 25:34-36).

() *Music.* Vocal and Instrumental. These gifts give a young person the potential and expertise to present a very personalized witness and inspiration to others through singing, or playing a musical instrument. (Psalm 96:1-9, Psalm 100:1-2, Psalm 149:1-2: Psalm 33:1-5, Psalm 150, I Samuel 16:14-23).

() *Pastoring.* A gift such as this gives a one the confidence, capability and compassion to provide spiritual leadership and direction for individuals or groups of believers. (1 Timothy 4:12-16, 1 Timothy 3:1-13, 2 Timothy 4:1-2).

() *Service.* This gift was originally called "helps." It is a gift that gives power to the young person to work behind the scenes in order that God's work is done. (Luke 23:50-54, Romans 16:1-16, Philippians 2:19-23).

() *Teaching.* This gift enables a young person to share a personal understanding of the Bible and religious issues in such a way that it becomes clear and understood by others. (1 Corinthians 12:28, Matthew 5:1-12, Acts 18:24-48).

() *Wisdom.* The gift that allows the believer to do critical thinking through understanding of various opinions, facts and thoughts in order to determine what solution would be best for others or the community of faith. (1 Corinthians 2:6-13, James 3:13-18, 2 Chronicles 1:7-11).

() *Writing.* A unique gift that gives a young person the skills necessary to express truth in a written form—one that can edify, instruct and strengthen others. (1 John 2:1-6, 12-14, 1 Timothy 3:14-15, Jude 3).

6. Become a discipler. We don't often use this term in this way. The Disciples of Jesus provide our model for this concept of involvement. We are all familiar with what it means to be a "teacher." We usually use this model of learning to get our own points across in a small group or study session. A religious education class may be the best illustration of this. We often sit in straight rows with someone of authority up front who is waxing eloquent on a topic he or she has just studied the night before. (This is, I hope, not typical, but nevertheless, it does happen). Being one who "disciples" others is slightly different, with different educational goals.

People, especially young ones, only know a "school model" for learning. They equate learning *anything* to their school experience, an experience that happens day in and day out. That makes teaching about life change difficult. You see, they bring to church the baggage and memories of the classroom.

If you are fortunate enough to have teachers in school that care about youth's religious growth, then you can build on that model, but since somewhere between 60 and 75% of the young people in local congregations go to public education, their understanding of school may be slightly different and their experiences may equally be good or bad, according to the expertise of the teacher, whether it be in Christian education or public.

So what is the difference? "Disciplers ask a different type of question regarding the goals of the teaching task. They ask, 'Am I preparing my students to be hearers of the Word or doers of the Word.'"[6]

Barry Gane, author and youth professional, defines discipleship with the following categories. "The new Christian's friend . . .needs to be a Christian model and spend time with the new Christian: discussing their spiritual lives, reading the Scriptures and praying, having fun-times together, seeking Christ-centered solutions to their problems."[7] As you can see, being a discipler takes more active compassion and focuses on different goals than those trying to get across "content" or "subject matter." In other words, fill your church with *mentors* of young people if we truly care to involve them in the life of the church, who can disciple them to a closer walk with Jesus. That is the chief goal of a discipler.

A mentor is one who guides, shares what they are excited about, models the types of behaviors and is open to share concerns and compassion. Mentors have great impact on the spiritual growth of the young. Helping involvement in the church is directly related to how many of your members feel attachment to the young people in the church. Being a good mentor is being a good discipler. John 15:12 in the discussion of the importance of being connected to the Vine says, *"My command is this: Love each other as I have loved you."* People don't care what you or I know until they know that we care. Our actions always speak louder than our words. People learn by our example. So before we can ever expect our children, friends, or anyone else to see our success, we must exhibit the other-focused characteristics of genuine love for others. That's what mentors do, and that is how disciples are taught to act.

Youth are always making judgments due to previous perceptions and earlier relationships. It is a simple equation. What they see, they become or react to. The Old Testament shares this same concern, and the Prophets of those times regularly called attention to the One who was driving their lives. They had their impact on the people. All of the membership of a local congregation share their view of God by their actions and their interest in the growing spiritual lives of the young.

If you want your youth to be involved, recruit mentors who can disciple your young people. Here is an activity you can use to encourage involvement of older people in the lives and cares of the younger members in your local church.

try this. *Secret Disciple.* Plan an event matching the young people of your church with an older person. Plan this from the adult side first and have members pick a "secret child" who becomes the disciple. Don't let the child know who you are and send birthday gifts, cards, flowers, or small gifts up to the day when you have a Secret Supper where everyone finds out who their "mentor" is when matched with the "disciple." This builds self-esteem and friendship and shows the young in the church that those older members care about the younger ones.

7. Be an equipper. I read somewhere about how hard it is to delegate responsibility. Many of us like to "do it all ourselves." But doing everything for our children or church members may be detrimental for growth in faith. After all, we have to understand just what we believe for ourselves. In faith-stage talk what is needed for a growing faith is *personalizing* that faith. This happens best in the early teen years as they begin to see things for themselves, make decisions for themselves and, at times, resent others telling them what to do, say, or believe. Our task is to equip our membership to be able to do for themselves, and "doing it" is always the beginning of commitment. Dave Stone's "Four Phases of Leadership" is helpful if we truly want to delegate and "equip" the youth of the church.

1. I do it, and you watch.
2. I do it, and you do it.

3. You do it, and I assist.

4. You do it, and I do something else.[8]

An easier way to say this targeted at teen ministry, is this paraphrase.

Step one: *I do it and you watch.*

Step two: *I do it, then you do it.*

Step three: *You do it and I support and supervise.*

Step four. *It's all yours kiddo!*

Any way you cut it, equipping others to be successful is a powerful way to ensure involvement. People become necessary and important when they contribute. Research on self-esteem shares that if you want to build it, give someone a task to accomplish. When it's completed and you step back and say, "I did that!" you begin to understand how you fit into the whole operation and how important your contribution to its completion really is. Equipping others is a wonderful skill for any congregation to master. Pastors who know how to delegate, members who know how to share, young people who see their importance are all central skills that increase involvement.

try this. *Involvement builder.* Try to do four of the following five activities next time you invite a young person to assist you in anything you do in the local church. Write these six suggestions down on a 3x5 card and keep them in your Bible so next time you see the young person that has helped you accomplish your task, you can encourage their excitement and motivate them to continue to be involved.

◦ Say something positive that makes them feel good about themselves.

◦ Tell them how much you appreciated their accomplishment

◦ Ask if they learned anything new in completing this task, and if so, have them explain what it was they learned. (Be attentive and listen).

◦ Let them know how much you appreciated their doing this on their own without too much help from anyone else.

◦ Ask them what they think they are good at and try to incorporate this skill or gift into the next challenge or task.

(Each of these questions is built on a list of factors that contribute to

people's excitement and motivation.)

Using these questions helps leaders encourage common people to accomplish uncommon things. Remember, people who are challenged to become great and are given the opportunity to do so, usually succeed.

8. Your faith-talk counts. One clear finding in the *Valuegenesis* research about family, church and school is that the amount of time spent sharing your own personal story about how God works in your life is time well spent in building strong faith in the lives of the children and youth who hear your story. We call it "Faith-Talk."

What is unique about this type of language is that it is not a testimony about God's goodness, even though we all have plenty to say about that! It is not even a telling of God's will for others, although it is always a temptation to tell others how to behave, what to believe, and how to decide. Instead, faith-talk is all about taking an opportunity to tell your story of how God works in your life and how He has led you in the past.

Most of the time we tell others what to believe or share some clarification of a theological point that we have found interesting, but if you truly want your church to master the art of faith-talk, then they must spend time thinking about God's work in their own lives. Then, take a moment to let someone else know what God is doing.

The Bible is filled with just that kind of talk. Joseph tells the story of his life and God's presence in it. Moses remembers what it was like living in Egypt, but yet still longs for a heavenly kingdom that brings true fulfillment to his soul. And Peter in the New Testament, even with his flawed character trait of always doing something wrong and then talking about it, eventually had his first chance to preach, and he talked about Jesus rather than himself.

Faith-talk is your sharing with young people God's rich goodness and action in your life. Involved youth in the church need to hear the stories of faith, stories that those who have lived lives in harmony with God's will and watched His working in their lives and in the lives of their own families can share.

Faith-talk works, and hearing these stories helps youth and young adults who are in their own way learning to see God's actions in their lives, understand the reality of the Christian walk.

9. Friendship is evangelism. One of the great goals of Adventism is to spread the gospel message around the world. Of course, it begins right at home. Before anyone can get involved in sharing, they have to feel comfortable sharing their own story. We've talked about helping adults learn faith-talk, but the same is true of young people as they develop their own story about God's work in their own lives. But sharing does not come easy.

In any life-cycle of a youth ministry, evangelism is always a later development. First you build a group, then you begin to fellowship together, have fun with each other, and begin to build a study group that cares about Scripture. Finally comes sharing. The best model for involvement of young people in the process of evangelizing one's community is to teach the youth how to make friends and through those relationships, invite them to come from outside of the church into new fellowship with people who care about them.

All too often we have a hook in what we do. For example, we feed people healthy food to get them interested in the church, with the motive of finally baptizing them. Or we hold meetings to give them new ideas about God's people based on sound exegesis and clear preaching. But the best method is using the common experience of friendship to bring young people to your church. And it works the other way too. If your church uses friendship to get young people involved, the church grows its teen ministry.

So the first task of any congregation is to find all of the youth that no longer attend and simply make friends with them all over again. Find people who they can relate with and get them talking and sharing together. Inviting them to become involved is a process of making friends. After all, what better way to learn to love Jesus than by having someone you just met care about you! Remember, fellowship *is* evangelism.

And to get your own youth involved in this process, you have to get them interested by being their friends. Any church that is judgmental and exclusive or even critical of things that young people care about is doomed to dwindle ministry to a standstill. So while you're caring about the environment, and building mentoring relationships and equipping them to help in the church using their gifts, given by God, take time to like them and know them.

31

try this. *Share a story of community.* Here is a story about a young student that just didn't learn that the church is a caring, loving group of people all on the same journey. Hear his story.

When I went away to a liberal arts college, I found it very difficult to maintain the faith that God had grown in me during junior high and high school As I lay in bed in my freshman dorm room, crying myself to sleep out of loneliness and lack of Christian friends, never once did I find solace in a funny story, clever anecdote, or gripping metaphor from my youth pastor's arsenal.

I must have heard 500 talks between 7th and 12th grades, counting Wednesdays, Saturday mornings and evenings, retreats, camps and mission trips—but I do not remember one of them as I was driven to new depths of doubt. Instead, I wondered if there was a God, and I tried unsuccessfully to read my Bible or to pray using the Adoration-Confession-Thanksgiving-Supplication system. I left high school ill equipped for my university experience. I had never really learned how to read the Bible, and I had never really learned how to pray, and I never really made good, lasting connections with the other students or adults in my church.

I was filled with knowledge, but without a community to shape and encourage me, I was lost.[10]

Ask your church board the following questions about their involvement in this youth's life.

() What could the church have done to build a community that would make sense to this young man?

() What are we doing that would make this kind of difference in our own congregation?

() What steps should we take to ensure this attitude does not exhibit itself in the youth of our church as they move to the university or community college experience?

10. Walking the talk. Consistency. That is what helps young people see the reality of the message of grace. For a denomination where cognitive understanding is crucial and doctrinal clarity is a mainstay, it is easy to see why this idea is so central. Our research shares that Adventist young people simply know their doctrines. In fact, almost all of the major beliefs of the Adventist church are clearly believed, no, definitely believed. And from 6th grade up their percentages of commitment to these beliefs don't change. That means first that we do a very good job of communicating to the youth of the church just what it is that Adventist believe. So belief in the teachings of the church is not at issue.

On the other hand, deep spiritual commitment that overflows in lifestyle and clear understandings and life choices is where we fail. Walking the talk is a crucial teaching method to cure this problem. As we are consistent with our beliefs in our behaviors, attitudes, speech, inclusiveness, and acceptance, young people will see that our lives are not just talk, but deeply changed by the power of God and Jesus' life, making up the difference in substitution for our natural ways.

Consistency is the only way that beliefs are translated into meaningful modes of practice and understanding for the young. After all, they look to adults and other significant people in their church to model what it really is like to be a Christian. And any church that doesn't take this lived-theology seriously is in for distance from their young people.

the jesus reason

One thing stands alone. It is not in our list of ten things to think about as you involve young people in the church. Instead, it is an over-arching principle that is central to the theology, mission, and motivation of anything religious. We exist, we thrive, we care because Jesus did it first. He models our thinking, behaviors and lifestyle. Without Him as the center of our reasons to become involved in the life and practice of the church, we've missed the mark by a long way.

Our theology of the doctrine of righteousness by grace through faith is in clear need of becoming as central to the mission and message of our local church as any other distinctive Adventist belief. His life and death become the real reason we do anything as a Christian. We just can't ignore this fact. Our reasons for being is because of His sacrifice for us in solving the problem of sin in the universe globally, and for saving us from its results personally.

The Jesus reason takes priority above any other belief or practice. And when young people come to realize His gift to us, their life changes as does the whole life and practice of a local congregation. "Christ first, last, and always," they say. In fact, those distinctive Adventist beliefs such as the remnant message, sanctuary understanding, and prophetic role of Ellen G. White continue to slip in importance with the youth of the church. The reason may be that we have forgotten how to place the message of salvation and the motivational life of Jesus right in the center of these crucial biblical truths. If we want to change this, we have to show how these specific beliefs make a difference in our lives. We have to show how these beliefs, along with everything else that Christians care about circle around our understanding of Jesus' message of love, compassion, and mission. This is a true challenge—to make the Jesus reason understood in everyone's life. It will take creative theology and insightful biblical understanding to accomplish this.

So what to do? Now comes the hard part, applying these principles to the very life of the local church. Everyone has a responsibility in this process. Pastors have to think about reorganization and leadership, parents must focus on building clear models of heaven in their homes and relationships, and local church leaders must begin to put into practice the things that make a difference.

Youth and young people are not left out either. They must be willing. Available. Trustworthy. All these characteristics of mature faith will serve them in good stead as they grow. So, what to do? Let's see what makes a difference. And as we look, take special care to evaluate your local congregation to see if you are doing any of the things suggested next. And if you are doing them, try to learn how to do them better and more Christ-centered. So lets do it and get on with involving young people in your own local congregation.

chapter 1 / endnotes

1. Complete information about the Valuegenesis research project can be found in the following two publications: V. Bailey Gillespie and Michael J. Donahue with Ed Boyatt and Barry Gane, *Valuegenesis—Ten Years Later: A Study of Two Generations* (Lincoln, NE: Advent*Source*, 2004) and Roger Dudley with V. Bailey Gillespie, *Valuegenesis: Faith in the Balance,* (Loma Linda University Press, 1992). These books are available at the John Hancock Center for Youth and Family Ministry, La Sierra University, Riverside, CA 92515 or by e-mailing hcyfm@lasierra.edu.
2. Les Parrott III, *Helping the Struggling Adolescent* (Grand Rapids, MI: Zondervan, 2000), 38-39.

3. Possible Responses to the Exercise in Active Listening adapted from Les Parrott III, *Helping the Struggling Adolescent*, 39-40.

1. I practice all the time, but it doesn't make any difference.—*Sounds as if you feel discouraged.*

2. Every other girl has a date but me.—*If feels as if you got left out.*

3. I shouldn't have slammed the door, but she shouldn't have said that.—*You feel kind of guilty but, at the same time, justified for what you did.*

4. I should be able to stay out past midnight if I want, Jim does.—*I wonder if you feel that your parents are being overly protective.*

5. Do you think I did the right thing?—*It sounds as if you're not very sure of yourself.*

6. I'd like to punch his lights out!—*You must be really angry.*

7. I don't want to talk about it anymore.—*It sounds as if you're feeling overloaded, as if it is all just too much.*

8. What's the use?—*As you say that, I get a picture of a guy who is discouraged and is crying uncle.*

9. What if she laughs at me? I'm not going to ask her.— *I get the sense that you're a little afraid and that your mind is made up.*

10. I don't feel anything about it.—*I'm wondering whether you have some idea of what you should be feeling and because you do not, you register it as not feeling anything.*

11. I don't believe that!—*I feel you are saying that you don't understand it, not really that you don't believe it.*

4. Jim Burns, Mike DeVries, *The Youth Builder* (Ventura, CA: Gospel Light, 2001), 108.

5. Used by permission and adapted from Neal Boese and Patricia Haller, Produced by the Education and Evangelism team of the Division for Congregational Ministries, ELCA. Copyright 1995 by the Evangelical Lutheran Church in America, Chicago, IL 60631 The original versions of this list of spiritual gifts are available 12/$12.00 from the ELCA Distribution Service along with a self-evaluation inventory of the gifts of the spirit.

6. Jim Burns, Mike DeVries, *The Youth Builder*, 110.

7. Barry Ganes, *Building Youth Ministry: A Foundational Guide* (Riverside, CA: Hancock Publications, 1997), 229.

8. J. David Stone and Rose Mary Miller, *Volunteer Youth Workers: Recruiting and Developing Leaders for Youth Ministry* (Loveland, CO: Group Books, 1985), 27-32.

9. For a complete discussion of these factors see James M. Kouzes, Barry Z. Posner, Edward Lawler III, and Patricia Renwick, *The Leadership Challenge* (San Francisco, CA: Jossey-Bass, Inc., 1995).

10. Adapted from Tony Jones, Postmodern Youth Ministry (Grand Rapids, MI: Zondervan, 2001), 82.

chapter 2

your church needs them

Once there was this church. Now, this church was like hundreds of others: it was shrinking and dying. Whenever a visitor dropped in to worship, they were left alone and were seen thumbing through the church bulletin trying to figure out what this "Doxology" was all about. No one bothered to tell them where it was in their church hymn book, and nobody ever thought to invite them home for a meal. They were seldom greeted, and after a couple of weeks, nobody seemed to know their names. After a few weeks they just felt isolated and disappeared. Very few of the regular members missed them; after all, they never truly saw them in the first place!

In this church, whenever a new family enters the church, they were often left to their own designs and initiative to find where the children's meetings were and just how to maneuver through the maze of hallways in the basement of the church. And when it came to the youth of the church, well, they just met in an old closet that usually had old papers and books stored inside. And during the cold winter—if you could believe it could get any colder—the members moved the youth out of their 'room" and they hung their dripping, sleet-covered coats in the same tight space.

On a scale of 1 to 10, how user-friendly would you say this church is to the visitors and especially to the youth of the church?

Of course, after that description, the question is really rhetorical, isn't it? In the day of hands-on computers, touch-screen iPads, iPods, do-it-yourself rebuilding, and picture phones, relational ministry, and post-modern young people, such a scenario is simply not consistent with the times or the conditions of relationships.

For young people, the church too often seems to lives in a time-warp of relevance. They think, "If it doesn't make sense, ignore it." "If it does not touch my life, forget it." And especially, "If the church—God's kingdom in verity—is not up-to-date, at least in terms of personal relationships, why would anyone want to come?" And joining and becoming a member there—well, for many, that is simply out of the question! The times of joining a church just because it seems to have a clear picture of God's truth, may very well be gone forever. Why join something that seems not to want you there?

This description and conclusion may seem a bit harsh, but to some degree, it is reenacted each week in many churches of all denominations. *We know from our Valuegenesis research that if a church learns to care in consistent, loving, and inclusive ways, the youth of that church will experience more positive feelings about that congregation, and struggling young people will see this fellowship as a place where they grow and learn.* In short, someplace where they would like to be. And if they feel accepted there, it makes it much easier for them to begin to clarify what they truly believe and establish a world view and a new set of clear beliefs.

why involvement is crucial

The phone rang on a hot July afternoon at my home. It was a local pastor who wanted some information from my denomination's research project.

"I have to preach a sermon this coming weekend, and I was wondering if you might help," he asked. I was flattered that someone wanted to learn something about the church.

"How can I get my young people involved in their own church? Can you give me a quick list of things that will work?"

I really wanted to help, but I wondered if I told that pastor the truth about what we found, how would he react and could he really change his church?

I asked, "What do you think are the barriers your church puts in front of the young people of your congregation?" He paused and had no idea how to answer.

What follows is a synopsis of what I believe are significant barriers to involvement in religion in general, and the church in particular. It is a fitting addendum to our last chapter of the ten most important things we just can't forget when we minister to the young in our congregations. Here is this list. The comments are mine, but the data of over 24,000 young people shares a powerful witness. Taking a clear look at what young people say about our religious life is a very important place to begin.

getting them involved. Here are some barriers to good ministry to young people in the local church.

1. *Lack of regular youth programming in the local church.* All too often churches view the young in its care as non-central to the life and ministry of the congregation. If this is the case, youth usually find some other place to be on the weekend. They go where the action is, and if your church doesn't have regular programming for preteens, teens, and young adults, then it is missing a powerful force for both ministry and help.

2. *Ignoring young people during worship services.* No one likes to be ignored. Young people, who by their very nature are struggling with identity issues and self-concept deficits, are extremely vulnerable. Their perception is the reality, and if the church does not recognize them, call them by name, or give them some status in the church, they are apt to find other places where this might happen. I want them involved in my church, and if this is a truism, then the church must find ways to include them intentionally.

3. *Thinking that all youth are alike.* Every one of the youth in your church are unique. They are not clones—even though their style seems duplicated over and over again in the looks of others of their age—in reality they are not all alike. Any church that deems involvement as crucial has to learn to accept the unique qualities of each young person. Jesus was often seen as someone who most would have considered an "outsider." But in reality, Jesus was the only true "insider" to the Kingdom of God. He demands care and compassion, identity and renewal in all those who want a place there. The young in the church deserve no less.

Just as Jesus' disciples each expressed individual characteristics and unique responses to His call, so the young in the church reflect individual personality and deserve individual care and ministry.

4. *Assuming that someone else will do youth ministry.* No. Everyone in the church is responsible for everyone else. Something about being "my brother's keeper," if I remember right. Jesus cleared this misconception up long ago as he told the story of the Good Samaritan. The church is to reflect the "example" of Jesus (1 Peter 2:21). So, don't wait until someone else does what you feel needs to be done. Everyone is a youth pastor. Everyone can mentor Christ's example and have an impact.

5. *If your church climate is not open, loving, and accepting, many youth just won't get involved at all.* We simply cannot say enough about this powerful variable in winning youth and involving them in their church. Unless the church is seen as warm and friendly, nurturing of a decisive thinking climate—one open to new ideas, ready to explore new questions and answers, along with acceptance of youth during times of doubt—most youth won't continue to see the local church as a viable source of spiritual life.

the potential within

I am sure you have heard people say that young people are the church of the future. And while this is true in one sense, in another it is absolutely false. Any message that youth are not now vital to the health and mission of the church is a false signal to their taxed identity development. Youth are a valuable resource right now in your church.

Much of what is wrong with youth stems from their view of themselves and from the projection that others send them about their lives. In psychological terms, this concept is called identity. And its formation is the topic of myriad forums, blogs, and articles. Famous for his understanding of youth identity was Erik Erikson, the father of identity theory.[1] This psychologist pioneered the concept of identity formation, and his insights are helpful when discussing the importance of youth involvement in value-laden enterprises.

An understanding of the term "identity" must be specifically established. Usually, the term has meant, in a commonsense way, "knowing where one fits." It is often called "personal identity" because it deals with how people feel about themselves. And this experience is often manifest in a gradual, moving or recurring sense of belonging and fit. For the social psychologist, identity is seen usually as a product of interaction with others in social settings.

But what does the formation of identity have to do with involvement in church? Well, for starters, look at this list of identity issues (Tags) that impact religious life. The connections are obvious because identity, then, means self-hood. Hans Mol argues that identity is, "anchored in a transcendent order symbolized in concepts and myths: less self-conscious than taken-for-granted."[2]

identity tags and church life

() Knowledge of one's place in the world.
() Feelings of acceptance and understanding.
() Experiences of success.
() A sense of accomplishment.
() An ordering of one's life.
() Feelings of fulfillment and purpose.
() A sense of knowing things will be OK.
() Understanding that one is needed.
() Unquestionable feelings of love.
() Experiencing the oneness with the universe.
() A sense of belonging and personal fit.

These all share a common denominator. All of the feelings or experiences listed above involve a knowledge of belonging and a clearing up of personal goals. This is what religion does in the life. When churches understand that whatever they do for and with their young helps build this sense of "other-worldly" acceptance and future, they will understand a key feature of religion in general. Religion gives us a home—a place where we are safe and where we can share eternal values. What more could we ask for our young people?

What does it take for the young people in the church, or for that matter all youth, to make it through these identity issues? What needs and experiences do they need that will reinforce their self's will to grow and to cope positively with the task of identity formation? One might say that within the context of Erikson's view of adolescence, four needs seem to be crucial:

(1) *Finding acceptance within community.* It is in the church community reflecting Christ's love and acceptance that youth find this need fulfilled.

(2) *Deepening interpersonal communication.* In a personal way the growing prayer life and study experience that the church can model provides a model of interpersonal relationships. And in a real sense, the fellowship of the saints can shape a response to this identity need.

(3) *Shaping an ideology or vision of life.* What better vision of life is there than the Christian ethic and beliefs? The need for an ideology is found through the growing awareness of one's own personal beliefs, and commitment to the Christian world-view provides a sense of mission and vision.

(4) *Achieving vocational direction.*[3] In biblical terms, people that found God began to "walk in the Way." This ordering of life's priorities and targeting a way to live serves as an identity function and again is met in one's commitment to God. All of these, all four, have a vital importance for identity formation, and through this formation, become the basis for understanding Christianity in a deep, real, and personal way.

The church as identity former then becomes a central factor to encourage commitment to the body of Christ. And just as surely as evangelism reaches out to the unchurched, fulfilling the identity needs of growing youth provides a unique evangelistic tool to encourage attachment to the visible body of Christ—His church and to God's people and their mission in the world.

the centrality of belonging

God's people have always been challenged to change. Scriptural passages which invite response are helpful in clarifying the beckoning of God. Such stories as the calling of the disciples, Moses, and Abraham all share a sense of how to respond to the vision God has for each life. So it is not a surprise that the early church saw evangelism and "call" as an important consequence of commitment.

And when anyone answers a call or responds to commitment they find themselves confronted with the possibility of change. And the direction of that change can often be toward personal involvement and acceptance in God's Kingdom. It is inevitable that a sense of belonging as a deep part of commitment will be the result.

All at once, the young person feels a part of something beyond him or herself. And like the conversion experience, this "new birth" brings a sense of ownership and fit. Thus, any way that the church or the youth ministry of a local congregation can strengthen this sense of fit and belonging will benefit the spiritual life of the young Christian, his and her church, vocation, and ultimately their religious life.

When the disciples were called, they *left* something and *found* something all at the same time. *Leaving* and *coming* are both important growth experiences that all who move through the cycle of life experience. They do so because of natural development and because of significant personal decision.

A sense of belonging makes understanding God's love easier. Since they personally feel that they belong to God due to the acceptance and involvement in God's work in the world, they deepen their commitment to both their church and their God.

try this. *Identity Study.* Here is a short Bible study that targets an understanding of identity and belonging. Give out the following texts, have the youth share these stories, and conclude by showing how their lives seemed different because of the decisions that these biblical characters made.
1. Exodus 12-13 - The story of the Passover.
2. 1 Kings 17:7-24 - The story of the Widow of Zaraphath.
3. Daniel 4-5 - Daniel's story in Babylon.
4. 1 Kings 10:1-13 - The visit of the Queen of Sheba.
5. Matthew 16 - The confession of Peter.
6. Matthew 10 - The healing of blind Bartimaeus.
7. Matthew 12:41-44 - The offering of the widow.
8. Mark 16:9-11 - Mary Magdalene sees Jesus in the Garden.

Spending some time trying to understand youth's feelings toward the church can prove to be a helpful activity for any group. Attitudes are formed through experience, and since the exposure young people have to their church forms a major part of their growing-up time, it is important, at least on occasion, to try to see just what feelings are being formed about this important institution.

If your local church and its multiple environments create such a positive impact on young people, then a sense of belonging is probably being nurtured. However, if the feelings young people have about their home or church are negative, then perhaps a distance is being created between their love for God and its expression in their lives. After all, young people want to *see* God and *feel* that power. If the environments where God is demonstrated do not reflect this reality, one might wonder what is really being learned. In educational circles we call this learning "incidental." We think we are teaching one thing, but in reality we are teaching something altogether different!

try this. *The Cup Church.* Take a Styrofoam coffee cup and give one to each young person. Give them some crayons or marking pens, some staples, pencils, thumbtacks, and miscellaneous other items that they could use to decorate their cups or have them simply express using the cup how they feel about the church. Give them about 20 minutes illustrate on their cups what they think of when they think of the word "church." See what happens and what comes out of the discussion you have about the nature of the term "church" by the young people of your local congregation. The time spent in debriefing their feelings may be quite revealing.

the power of the family

On the other hand, you might want to explore another specific venue for ministry—the family. More and more research is telling us to realize the fact that good youth ministry implies a clear understanding of family ministry.

For years, many involved in church ministry took an almost anti-family approach. "Hey, look how these parents have fouled up their kids," or, "Now we have to straighten out 15 years of damage done by the parents." Many youth ministries saw themselves as "counter-forces to families."[3] Now, of course, we know that there is power in the family as an essential element in nurturing a Christian world-view. Family ministry is an important adjunct in the church ministry for young people. That is why any good ministry in church models the ministry that should be taking place in the home. Family ministry is essential and crucial.[4]

Ideally, the family's sense of acceptance and fit will be reflected in the church and visa versa. However, often there are conflicts between the home and the church. Youth are often more inclined to share their problems with church workers than their parents. They often feel more comfortable talking to their teachers or pastors than their parents. This dissonance stresses the importance of accepting, non-judgmental environments where the grace of God can be seen. Youth that face this conflict often have a difficult time in seeing the church as accepting. Getting the parents involved in youth ministry is important. Develop your parents as an extension of your church's ministry to the young. Then both the church and the family are benefited.

There seems to be a direct correlation between the amount of parental gripes about the church's ministry for youth and the amount of information they have. So it is important for the ministry in the church to include parents in clarification of the needs they have regarding the ministry to their own children. Here is a questionnaire that can be used to help parents focus on their own needs and can be used to inform the ministry of the local church in order to enhance the communication between the church's ministry and that of the families of the young in the church.

try this. *Parent Survey.* Here is a confidential survey for parents of high school students. Using it will help your ministry be relevant and considerate of the needs of the parents of the youth in your church.

Instructions: Please help us make the ministry at our church the very best it can be. We want to serve yo and your young people. Please take a moment to complete this brief questionnaire and return it to the youth ministry office by next week. Your responses will be kept in strict confidence. *(You may wish to make an on-line survey for use on the World Wide Web, there are a number of free services available for you to use if you do some searching).*[5]

(Score between 1 and 6 with 1 being strongly agree and 6 being strongly disagree) Please be as honest as possible as you answer these question. Thank you for assisting us with this survey.

1. Our youth ministry at our church helps my child feel loved.

Strongly agree   Strongly disagree

1   2   3   4   5   6

2. The youth ministry makes my child feel needed.

Strongly agree   Strongly disagree

1   2   3   4   5   6

3. Our youth ministry meets my child's needs.

Strongly agree   Strongly disagree

1   2   3   4   5   6

4. Our youth ministry uses my child's talents and abilities.

Strongly agree   Strongly disagree

1   2   3   4   5   6

5. Our youth ministry seems to be for a select few.

Strongly agree   Strongly disagree

1   2   3   4   5   6

6. Our youth ministry helps my child's faith grow.

Strongly agree   Strongly disagree

1   2   3   4   5   6

7. Our youth ministry informs me of what is going on.

Strongly agree   Strongly disagree

1   2   3   4   5   6

8. Youth ministry asks too much from parents.

Strongly agree   Strongly disagree

1   2   3   4   5   6

9. Our youth ministry enhances our family relationships.

Strongly agree   Strongly disagree

1   2   3   4   5   6

10. Our youth ministry has helped my child.

Strongly agree   Strongly disagree

1   2   3   4   5   6

the ministry of interpersonal communication

Involvement in the church is not just participation in and creation of a sense of belonging. It can take on many more multiple faces. And just as surely as it is active participation, it can be passive reflection too. As any parent knows, opportunities to talk come in various ways and during unexpected encounters. Communication about God and involvement in His plan can take place at some rather odd times. One aspect of youth ministry often overlooked is the beauty of the chance encounter.

I was sitting on a plane traveling to the east coast and was watching to see who would be sitting in the middle seat next to me, hoping that it would be empty on this long cross-country flight. Right at the last minute, Carol walked in. She was dressed all in black. Black fingernails. Long silver ear studs that matched her bracelets. And safety pins clinging to her worn Dickey pants. My first impression was, "Wow!" I wonder what she is like.

After take-off, I ventured a weak "hello," then waited. She responded in clear English telling me she was going home after spending the summer in Germany. I asked if her parents would be surprised to see her. She said, "Yes, wouldn't you be surprised to see me?"

After some time she shared with me her adventures traveling around Europe, her meeting with a group of Christians, studying her Bible, learning to pray, and sharing with me how she had become a Christian.

Now, she didn't look like most of the Christian young people I worked with on my university campus, but after some time together, she shared her plan on a career in the health professions as an expression of her commitment to mission. She was going home to talk to her parents and share her good news with them. For more than two hours we examined our respective pilgrimages, questioning, and commenting until our mutual sharing drew us together as spiritual partners.

Thinking back on this encounter much later I was reminded of Ross Snyder's concept of the "Great Conversation," a conversation between an adult and a youth that I had reviewed in my doctoral program at Claremont Graduate University back in the early '70s.[6] Snyder shares that this conversation "may be an exploration of such themes as love and freedom; it may begin by reflecting upon the meaning of a book or movie; it may focus upon a disclosure of truth that has given one deepened self-understanding and a fresh sense of direction to life."[7] He reminds us that on such occasions the adults initially serve as midwives to the "birthing" of "rich and resolute inwardness," but in listening and becoming an eventual partner in this conversation, the adults too are inwardly enriched. Snyder adds that such conversation can occur in a group with one or more adults engaging the interests and concerns of their young people.[8]

The ministry of interpersonal communication is a wonderful way to begin to involve young people in the life and mission of their church and their vision of God's plan for their lives. Your "Great Conversations" with young people may lead to important shaping of their decisions and values, and a reorganization of your own.

Involvement takes many shapes and forms. It can be as direct as encouraging young people to take part in a particular program at church. It may include early-on such things as participation and observation of adult roles in the church, or it may be much more subtle.

Involvement might mean learning to ask important questions, or finding out the resources that could enrich one's answer. Involvement may be very personal rather than a corporate experience. It could look like contemplation and withdrawal, or it may mean active participation in a mission or project of the church and may simply include the casual encounter with a significant adult or young adult in the church as the youth explores his or her deep concerns about life.

try this. *Great conversations Try-out.* Plan to meet two young people this weekend. If you are in church, see if you can just meet someone new—learning their names gives them some sense of identity and belonging—so take a moment to learn the names of two of your youth and just say "Hi!" Remember, don't talk to them, or about them, only talk about your own relationship to God. Share a quick insight you received, or something about your own experience with God when you were younger and then listen to them. Don't be aggressive, don't be preachy, don't try to get any point across, try to just have a brief conversation with a young person in your church and listen to what they have to say. See if this evolves into one of those "Great Conversations" mentioned above.

get involved when it is natural

While it is important to look for opportunities to involve young people in interpersonal communication, there are special times when opportunities to communicate are most natural and involvement in the lives of the young are most common.

There are times when planned relationships are peculiarly significant. During periods of natural transitions and developmental crisis communication is easiest and most helpful. Youth ministry has often used these natural times to initiate discussions with young people, but becoming expert in knowing when these times are helps these "identity conversations" along.

When youth "come of age" and begin to take on the responsibilities of young adulthood are natural times when communication with youth must be initiated and sustained.

Good parenting dictates that you keep open the channels of discussion during these troubling times, especially if one wants to make a difference. Pastors, teachers, parents, professional youth ministers in most churches can use these times to learn how to make an impact on young people's faith lives.

One might want to initiate the adaptation of Donald McNassor's rationale and model for high schools. Educator McNassor discovered in his research in school counseling that students in their senior year react with anxiety as they approach the day of graduation. He reports, "One is struck by the kind of tranquilized mood the students have created for themselves . . . They seem partially paralyzed for action such as talking with people, making inquiries and specific plans. They are waiting, waiting for what they call the big change to come."[9]

identity moments. So, what are the moments when change is most natural? Here is a list of possibilities for involvement in the life of a young person.

- () Birthdays
- () Graduations
- () Moving days
- () First drivers license
- () Sporting awards
- () Class honors
- () Class offices
- () Report card days
- () Mission trips
- () Intercity helping projects
- () First day of school

() Academic honors

() New family member (brother/sister)

() First date

() Death in the family or of a friend

() Baptism

() Participation for the first time in the adult church

Can you think of other natural times when change or crisis happens?

the role the church

Recent research by the Barna Group looking at the shifting landscape of youth ministry in major denominational churches has noticed a unique trend emerging. Some "six out of 10 teens involved in a church probably will not continue their spiritual commitment into early adulthood."[10]

This study, conducted from 2001 to 2006, affirmed what we had suspected in our own *Valuegenesis* research on Seventh-day Adventist teens. Our research showed high levels of spiritual activity during these early years. And over a ten-year period between studies, their level of spirituality increased extensively. This is due to quality ministry to this age group in churches and schools, and the fact that developmentally teens are receptive to matters of faith due to their own personal willingness to deal with issues of character, curiosity to try new things, and the issues of identity formation extant during these years.

But as teens grow older, something happens. During the early years when the church tries to plan ministry for youth, the results are positive because of renewed emphasis and the occasion of many thriving youth ministries. But according to Barna's research, the disengagement among 20-somethings suggests that ministry to this age fails too often at discipleship and faith formation. Hannah Elliott, commenting on this research says, "The point is that the current state of ministry to 20-somethings is woefully inadequate to address the spiritual needs of millions of young adults."[11]

What is the solution to this lack of involvement of these young adults? It seems that some solutions are obvious.

1. *Make sure that your youth ministry has a wide perspective and naturally moves teens into their young adult years with the care and ministry of the local church if you want consistent involve-*

ment in your church. If your church does not have a young adult ministry, make sure someone sees this as their mission and develop these natural transitions into ministry opportunities. There are in the life-cycle of young people two major transitions times. Our research shows teens are especially vulnerable during the 8th grade to 9th grade transition, as well as the high school to college or the work-place transition.

This is a logical chance to stress the power of Christian educational experiences. If higher education is your teen's goal, move them to a Christian college, encourage their involvement, and support their decisions to go on student missions, community service outings, and on-campus religious activities. Christian schools can be a major help in these transition times, and their impact goes well beyond just the academic advantages. If youth are in public education, engage them in a church club or begin one yourself. If your church has a university or college nearby, just contact the student life office and see what rules there are for ministry on that campus. But do something to bridge the gap between high school and higher education.

2. *Be intentional and wholehearted about focusing on helping teens learn commitment, passion, and resources that guide their lives if you want them involved.* We can never say enough about passing on the mission and passion of Jesus to the next generation.

3. *Being personal is best.* According to Elliott again, if you want long-term involvement, try to "become more personalized in your ministry to these older adults. Since everyone has different needs, questions and doubts, help them to wrestle through those specific issues and to understand God's unique purpose for their lives."[12] Again, try to build a personal ministry. As faith becomes personalized itself, it takes on the flavor and interests of the young person. Here is a chance to guide and point to biblical examples of faith life, your own personal challenges and victories, and build a community of caring, grace-oriented people that can continue this friendship after they leave the confines of the local church. Too often we forget their young people after they leave the church. If they come back, they remember them, but if they are gone and away from the ministry of their local church, it is even more important to find ways to communicate with them in a personal way.

4. *Unless the ministry to the teens and young adults provides*

a biblical viewpoint and a process for establishing biblical values,
they will have a difficult time as they make their own responses to
life's challenges after they leave your care. Making decisions in light
of God's will is a maturing faith challenge and one that parents and
youth workers must take seriously.

5. *Keep using Jesus Christ as your model of behavior and passion.* If you want involvement during these life transitions, we have
to give young people a reason to be what they might not normally
choose to be. Spending the majority of your time on behavioral
issues, church traditions, antiquated rituals or meaningless worship
will shift their attention from what is crucial. Somehow we must
give the youth of the church a vision of the reason that the church
exists. They must know that Jesus Christ is the sole reason for being and behavior. That the life and ministry of Christ exemplifies
what Christianity must become. That the will of God is best see in
the works of Christ. And that a relationship with the God of the
universes comes naturally through close, passionate commitment
to God's son, Jesus—the ONE. Somehow, all too often we miss
this vision and replace it with the politics of the local church or the
traditional concerns of people that have missed this vision. So talk
of the great things God can do. Spend time focusing on the mission of Christ in the world, sharing the nature of God's Kingdom
people. Study together what God's will might be for each young
person in your care in light of what Jesus did for us.

"I believe that the youth of today have wonderful potential for
being the strong and vibrant church leaders of tomorrow," says
Gar Micklelson in his article, "Are Church Teens Going to Pot?"[13]
He says this because he sees in youth a desire to express the love of
Jesus in real ways to others. And sharing God's love has a profound
effect.

You want youth involvement in your church? Ask the tough
questions and then reflect on your own personal response.

() Do you represent God's actions in the world and can model
them for the youth of your church?

() Does your youth and young adult ministry reflect the big issues that Jesus came to share in the world—fairness, equity, equality, integrity, love and compassion?

() Do you take the time to let your church know of its responsibility to the whole life cycle of the young in your charge—preteens,

teens, 20-somethings?

() Do you help build strong family ministry in your church?

() Do your ministry and concerns reflect respect for the individual faith development of each and every young person and is it sensitive to the ways in which each learn?

These questions are difficult and their answers are very personal. But together, as we keep our eyes fixed on the author, perfecter, and finisher of our faith, we will begin to see the power of Christ's influence in both our lives and in the lives of our young people. We have wonderful young people and their involvement is crucial to the church's present and future.

chapter 2 / footnotes

1. Erik H. Erikson, *Childhood and Society* (New York: Norton, 1950), 242.
2. Hans J. Mol, *Identity and the Sacred* (New York: Free Press, 1976), 59.
3. Thom Schultz and Joani Schultz, *Involving Youth in Youth Ministry: A New Way to Help Kids Take Responsibility* (Loveland, CO: Group Books, 1987), 38.
4. See, V. Bailey Gillespie, Judith Gillespie, Tim Gillespie, Cheryl Webster, *Keeping the Faith: A Guidebook for Spiritual Parenting* (Lincoln, NE: AdventSource, 2002). This guidebook with Parent Potentials provides hundreds of ideas for families to build a spiritual life and stresses the power of clear family ministry in the local church.
5. Adapted from Thom Shultz and Joani Schultz, *Involving Youth in Youth Ministry*, 41-41.
6. Ross Shyder, *Young People and their Culture* (Nashville, TN: Abingdon Press, 1969), 160-162.
7. Reflections on Synder's "Great Conversations" by Paul B. Irwin in *The Care and Counseling of Youth in the Church* in the Creative Pastoral Care and Counseling series edited by Howard J. Clinebell, Jr., (Philadelphia, PA: Fortress Press, 1975), 35.
8. Ross Snyder, *Young People and Their Culture*, 162.
9. Donald McNassor, "Seminar Working Paper, No. 2, "Seeing Through a Glass Darkly: Outer Edges of Identity in the Seventeenth Year of Life," (Claremont Graduate School & University Center, Claremont, CA, 1960-61), 2.
10. George Barna, The Barna Update, "Most Twenty-somethings Put Christianity on the Shelf Following Spiritually Active Teen Years," (Ventura, CA: The Barna Group, September 11, 2006), 1-7. Accessed on 10/27/06 at <http://www.barna.org/FlexPage.aspx?Page=BarnaUpdate&BarnaUpdateID=245>.
11. Hannah Elliott, Associated Baptist Press, Ventura, CA. "Many U.S. Teens Losing Faith by Early Adulthood." Accessed on 10/26/2007 at <http://www.westernrecorder.org/wr/wrsite.nsf/stories/200638-TeenFaith. 1>.
12. Hannah Elliott, "Many U.S. Teens Losing Faith by Early Adulthood," 2.

chapter 3

getting rid of myths and sacred cows

before we get too far in this book, I think that we should tackle some difficult issues regarding ministry for and with young people. If we really want them to get involved in the church, we have to take a good, clear, and logical look at the *kind* and *type* of ministry we perceive as essential to nurture committed, Christ-centered involvement.

We have all been confronted with some things that simply are not true when it comes to caring for young people. We all have some misconceptions about them. We remember the way it *was* and it was *always* better.

One young youth professional was asked to organize a youth ministry in a mid-sized, urban church. They had not had a very successful ministry before he came. His challenge—find the youth, get them involved, help them to grow, and in the long-term, to help them meet Jesus as their personal friend.

His ministry grew very slowly. Two-thirds of the churched youth were in public education, not the church school nearby, so it was hard to get access to them and to fit the church schedule into their already busy school schedules of sports, plays, music practice, and family chores. The church school had its own schedule with Bible studies, chapels, sharing, sports, plays, and music appointments too. But he tried, and after three years he had grown a ministry from about 12 young people to 45-65 teens on any given week. During the summers the ministry was much stronger,. After all, school was out, and both church schooled and public schooled youth found time for the same kinds of activities. The Tuesday night concerts with contemporary bands and pastor-led Bible study grew his group to around 80 young people on most Tuesday nights.

The senior pastor was older, and from another country. He remembered when he had a youth-focused ministry back home—a ministry in a different time and different country. But it was successful, about 200 young people each week, he claimed. He dropped discouraging bombshells in the lap of this young pastor. Not real criticisms, but enough concern to make the young pastor feel he was not able to do a good job, especially when this senior pastor suggested he take over the young adults as he knew how to be successful.

Eventually, this growing, discouraging input caused self-doubt. The youth pastor finally accepted a call somewhere else. Even though his ministry was exciting, growing, and based on sound theological and educational principles, he just had to leave.

Looking back now, that church really has not had as dynamic a ministry since, but the discouragement was real and caused personal concern for the young pastor. It contributed to his decision to find another ministry that would better match his gifts.

The older pastor was operating within a myth. His memory was better than reality. He had made his ministry a sacred cow because no one would ever do it right or just the way he had done it.

I believe there are a number of myths and sacred cows that need some work. If you are a youth professional, you have had to deal with some or all of these issues before. If you are a religion teacher, you meet these concepts at regularly scheduled intervals. If you are a parent and a concerned church member, you have seen this kind of discouragement before. These sacred cows are often frustrating when confronted, because people believe that things should not change or innovation is somehow *bad*, if not down-right evil.

Let's look at some myths and sacred cows [something too highly regarded to be open to criticism or curtailment] that just might need to be corrected, forgotten, or killed before your church can get their young people truly involved in the vision of your church.

sacred cow no. 1: believing that your own model of youth ministry is the only one that will work best.

While often the status of youth ministry in the church can be described as chaotic and confused, and while many people in the church as well as local youth leaders are productive and fruitful, trying to survey the lay of the land as to the best ways to do ministry to young people is often futile. Churches have tried everything, but to no avail. Their young people's ministry seems to struggle along, crippled by lack of participation and wounded by inconsistent leadership.

Tim Neufeld, a Christian youth professional says, "Across North America youth leaders and pastors are asking, 'Why is youth ministry not working like it has in the past?' For decades youth ministry has been patterned after, and comfortable with, one or two basic models of operation, but with the onset of the post modern culture those models are no longer valid. 'What do we do now?' cry leaders in the new millennium."[1]

The reality is that there is no longer just one right way to do it. There are lots of reasons for this. Some argue that the culture has shifted. Others believe that youth are just too difficult and self-absorbed to want God or the church.

Where we once were a "church" culture with everything in the community revolving around one's local church, now the values of our society often don't include church life, and many youth and even more young adults don't seek out the church on their own initiative. Some don't even view the church as relevant or helpful. The conclusion? Now we live in an "unchurched culture."[2]

In order to refute this first sacred cow, we need to clarify just how this culture might be different in order to successfully minister to it. Tony Jones in his book on *Postmodern Youth Ministry* argues that there really is a difference now. He summarizes his discussion by sharing words commonly found in this youth culture like secularism, pluralism, relativism, existentialism, individualism, and materialism. From his perspective, and probably from a correct one, he suggests the postmodern credos include such things as objectivity or thinking (out), subjectivity or feelings (in). He says this culture questions everything and doubts if there is anything that is "Truth" with a capital "T." He describes the youth of this post modern time as those who tell stories and never make lists.[3]

Youth is a culture that, like Leonard Sweet says, highlights the acronym EPIC: the new culture is *"Experiential, Participatory, In-*

teractive, and *Communal.*"[4] All these attributes add to our confusion as to how to involve young people in the life and mission of the church. It is a new age and in many ways new approaches and models must be explored if we want to get the most potential out of the ministry of Christ in the church of today.

There are many models to explore for the local church. Here is a brief summary of the choices. But you can't keep up with the models; they are changing as rapidly as the lives of the young.

check out these youth ministry models.

You might want to place a check mark by some selected models that you think might work in your own situation. There may be more than one to use, based on your mission and goals. I have provided a brief description of the model and its basic goals.

❏ **purpose driven youth ministry**—Made famous by Doug Fields.[4] Follows the progress from evangelism, discipleship, fellowship, ministry and worship. Its focus is to equip students rather than a ministry that coordinates events. It incorporates an incarnational youth ministry theology.[5]

❏ **incarnational youth ministry**—Just as Jesus took the form of a human being, we must take on the "form" of a young person through close human contact, loving relationships that we take very seriously, for they are a place where we can find God, and grow in our own relationship with God.[6]

❏ **relational youth ministry**—Through our relationships with youth, we help them discover God in their relationships and grow as well. By building these relationships with youth we bring them into communion with the whole community of faith and in that context work with them on their issues and development. The church's role is to show authentic concern for young people. Building community is one solid purpose of this model.[7]

❏ **the nucleus model of youth ministry**—The most common model of ministry to "churched" young people. Built around a youth fellowship approach, its aims are to nurture young people in the Christian faith and to share this message to others outside of the fellowship group. It is the basis for many church youth associations and church clubs. The strategy is carried out by building a youth group already affiliated with the church, helping them build faith, and encouraging them to bring their non-Christian friends to the meetings or to special evangelistic events.[8]

❑ **the wedge or growth model of youth ministry**—A rather formal model of church ministry to the young people. It argues for a relational ministry by those in charge of youth programming with an evangelistic approach to move youth to a time of recognition of what they have learned to believe. It stresses the memberships responsibility for a continuous approach to the youth and then emphasizes the church's responsibility in educating the young in the tenants of the faith, doctrines, and behaviors. It reflects a model that begins early in life and grow until a time of "recognition."[9]

❑ **the comprehensive model of youth ministry**—For lack of a better title, we call this the "comprehensive" model. It is called that, because it is. It includes as much as you can cram into your programming, activities, involvement, and study. It has a broad scope. Beyond youth group programming, it emphasizes multiple program formats using a large number of contents offered in a variety of time formats and settings. The goal is to broaden the total participation of young people because followers of this model believe that young people go where the action is, and where their interests lie. It is characterized by balance among components, variety of program formats and schedules, multiple environments where programs take place, including the church, home, retreat centers, community centers, youth centers, and interest-centered programming. In this model youth have real freedom to choose what works for them in a small group format with multiple adult mentors.[10]

In light of these classic youth ministry models, and there are others we could cite.[11] Four typologies (types of ministry) have been identified through analysis of most of the approaches of ministry to young people. Mark Senter in his book, *Four Views of Youth Ministry,* enters into dialogue with four proponents of these styles of ministry and asks the following questions to those contemplating such work with youth:

◊ *Inclusive congregational* (Malan Nel). What happens when a church thoroughly integrates its adolescents, making them full partners in every aspect of congregational life?[12]

() *Preparatory* (Wesley Black). Why and how should a church consider its teenagers as disciples-in-training and its youth ministry a school of preparation for future participation in church life?[13]

() *Missional* (Chap Clark). What does a church look like, whose youth ministry does not necessarily nurture "church kids" but is essentially evangelistic? Whose youths and youth workers are considered missionaries?[14]

() *Strategic* (Mark Senter). How feasible is it for a youth ministry to become a new church on its own—the youth pastor becoming the pastor, and the new church planted with the blessing of the mother church?[15]

to walk you must start

The first step in ministry to young people involves finding your passion (mission and vision); identifying the needs of the youth in your church and community; beginning to grow a ministry through grace-filled acceptance, biblical study, personal understanding, community service, and action. Trying to find a balance is the challenge.

There is more to come on this topic later in this book, so remember the term "balanced" ministry model whenever you think seriously about involving young people in the life of your church. It always takes more than one way to do ministry to the young, so don't accept the sacred cow of one size fits all! Tim Neufeld, a youth ministry professional, summarizes this sacred cow this way. "One thing is clear from reading [new publications for youth ministry professionals]: youth ministry will never again have a common methodological approach as it did in the previous century."[16]

sacred cow no. 2: just one hour a week is enough if we want to make a difference.

You do the math. According to the A.C. Nielsen Co., the average American watches more than 4 hours of TV each day (or 28 hours/week, or 2 months of nonstop TV-watching per year). In a 65-year life, that person will have spent 9 years glued to the tube.[17]

If you follow the statistics closely regarding children, they watch television 1,680 minutes per week. That totals over 1500 hours that the average American youth watches television as contrasted with a total of only 900 hours that these youth spend in school. Young people see over 20,000 30-second commercials a year. The average child, "will watch 8,000 murders on TV before finishing elementary school. By age eighteen, the average American has seen 200,000 acts of violence on TV, including 40,000 murders. Dr. Jon Nelson of the American Medical Association said that 2,888 out of 2,000 studies show that TV violence is a casual factor in real-life mayhem. It's a public health problem. The American Psychiatric Association addressed this problem in its endorsement of National TV Turnoff Week, stating, "We have had a long-standing concern with the impact of television on behavior, especially among children."[18]

Contrast this secular involvement with the religious exposure of an average Christian teen. Perhaps 3 hours a week—and that's pushing it—time spent with some exposure to religious life. And if your church only occasionally has a youth meeting, or some form of activity for specific age groups, then the exposure is even more limited.

being like christ takes some time

If you are serious about spiritual life, you have to take time. time for renewal, time for questioning, time for reflection, time for discipling. And if one of your goals is to move young people from just being spectators to active participation, we have to recognize that one hour a week just won't cut it.

Discipleship means getting kids involved! "The bottom line in youth work is not how many kids are coming to your youth ministry right now. The bottom line is where your kids will be five to ten years from now. How are you preparing them to be lifelong followers of Jesus Christ? How are you preparing them to be Christian leaders?"[19] This quotation by Jim Burns comes from years of helping youth become involved in local church life. He goes on to suggest that contrary to some of the most contemporary philosophies of ministry to the young, becoming a mature disciple of Christ simply never comes by memorizing a manual or taking some course offered in five evenings in a local church. Really becoming a child of God simply is never a program one graduates from. In fact, he claims, the process of becoming faithful is not about knowledge transfer at all; it's "about life transformation. It is a long-term, character-building relationship that challenges people to take what they have been given by our Lord and share it with others."[20]

After all, the Christian life is just that, a life, one dedicated to God. And that means long-term exposure and habit formation along with renewing commitment and dedication. These traits don't come after one hour of church or an occasional youth meeting.

Many church leaders bemoan the fact that youth seem to be leaving the church. Some leave in droves after a high school experience, others drift away because they have never seen other religious people care about them long-term. So this sacred cow is gone! If you want young people involved, you have to start to commit both time and energy, long-term renewal of your church, and some quality time with all of the young in your church. An eternity is a long time to be with people that you've never thought cared enough to invite you to become a friend of God.

sacred cow no. 3: thinking that these young people are not as committed to god as we were when we were young.

This sacred cow really needs killing. Sure, people change, and some people change some of the time. But research has always indicated just how crucial the teen and young adult years are in establishing both one's ideology (belief system) and ones identity (ownership by God). Adolescence is a natural time for change. In fact, most of the religious conversion research shares that adolescence is the prime time for religious commitment, and, in fact, if that change doesn't happen in these years, it very well may not happen at all. [20]

Since youth is a time when change might occur, it is logical to believe that commitment should be evident at this age. Our memories are not very good as we get older, and remembering what you were like when you were young now that you are older is probably not too reliable.

We do know that young people go through the same process everyone does to make decisions and evidence change. And, in working with religious change, we are not alone. The Holy Spirit is a partner with us as the Spirit's love is seen in the relationships built between adults and young people. Chap Clark and Kara Powell in their book, *Deep Ministry in a Shallow World,* share the startling revelation that, "ministry to young people is really seeking to persuade them, without an agenda demanding a response, to consider who God is and what his call is for their lives." They quote (2 Corinthians 5:11, TNIV), "We try to persuade people" as a truism in ministry to youth. [22]

A deeper goal in ministry to the young would be to convince them that God does the changing and they only need to be receptive and receive God's call. Commitment is the result of this process. It is no different than the decisions we once made, and their result in young people's lives is just as exciting and life-changing as it was when we first heard of the Gospel and God's graceful gift of love.

Some of the professional models of youth ministry stress commitment. Mark Tittley developed this model of youth ministry to insure that newcomers are added to the group, and that those already within the group are matured in their faith and equipped to serve. This spiritual growth model fits well into the other models of ministry we've explored, but these and others that could be used by local congregations all have one purpose.[23] That purpose is to grow faithful Christians that reflect God's grace and have a commitment to serve.

This sacred cow #3 is simply not true. Youth become committed just as we did, and they do it with the same regularity and decisiveness as ever before. Even the earliest research on conversion argues that this age group to a larger extent than the general adult population experience change. In our research, 44% of over 22,000 young people from grades six through twelve in church schools across the United States said that their commitment to Jesus came over time, while only 13% of these same students said that their decision to follow Jesus came at a specific time. 32% said that this decision came during their youth, and almost all saw themselves as religious.

Commitment seems to come regularly during the time of

youth, and the church should take this into consideration and recognize just how crucial their ministry to the young is during this timely decision-making process.

sacred cow no. 4: size really does matter.

Anyone who has worked in a local church with a ministry with young people knows about this sacred cow. It comes from a natural human concern to be successful. When we were students and we wrote a term paper, seldom was anyone interested in our topic. We knew this, because the questions we got from classmates were always about the length of the paper, seldom the content.

As a teacher at a major university for decades, I have heard and seen it all. But one common flaw in education is the desire for students to feel successful simply because they have done their assignment. From a professor's vantage point, we want to believe that learning for learning's sake is the real motivator. The love of learning is the purpose for schools. So we think. But after a few years of the grind of classroom assignments and grading, we recognize that often the size of the product is perceived as more crucial than contents. The medium is the message. The box is often more expensive than the present.

The size of your group, or the number of people that attend a given meeting or outing, all too often becomes the criterion for excellence. And all too often we realize that we are truly in a numbers game. My meetings had 2,000 youth. Well, mine, had 9,000. And meetings are often judged successful by their size, and like term papers, seldom seen as needing to have deep, spiritual content.

But size does matter. Yes. On occasion, when one of your goals is to get everyone involved, size often does matter. Size doesn't matter, however, when you talk of quality. One young person totally committed to loving God and changing his or her choices to reflect a Christian world view is more valuable than hundreds at the youth rally, and thousands at the prayer conference.

So in the midst of living with the reality of the size matters cow, remember the parable of the lost sheep, the lost coin, and the lost prodigal son. Jesus said that, simply put, everyone is valuable to God's Kingdom. Just one would have sent the wheels of heaven in motion towards salvation. One lost sheep causes the shepherd to rethink his priorities. Yes, he has the whole herd still coming to the watering hole, but one—just one is enough to change the priority of the shepherd and cause him to brave the cold and wind to find that one lost.

So what is the message to the church about this sacred cow? Remember the parables. Reform your ministry to find those outside the shelter of your church. Care for the whole, but don't forget the uniqueness and individuality of every young person in your church because size doesn't really matter when it comes to making personal choices. Rededicate your church to the mission of helping one youth at a time and watch how it impacts the whole congregation.

sacred cow no. 5: all it takes for good ministry to young people is an outgoing and charismatic leader.

The cult of personality is what plagues this sacred cow. And its myth professes that regardless of content, programming skills, organization, planning and visioning, in the long run, all young people want is someone to inspire them and lead them somewhere.

Now, it is true, however, that when the other aspects of professional and competent ministry are absent in a local congregation, personality goes a long way in building some sort of ministry. But even though this is a possibility, any ministry that runs solely on personality and gifts is sure to eventually be devoid of purpose and longevity. When the person goes, so goes the ministry. And all-too-often churches are left with a floundering program for ministry because their key people are now gone.

Remember, young people's ministry includes aspects of passion and belonging. It is both exciting and educational. Ministry to the young presupposes that those involved have a multitude of gifts and ability to touch every aspect of young life. In Carol Lytch's book, *Choosing Church: What Makes a Difference for Teens,* she observes that for many teenagers, faith development and involvement in a congregation is still a matter of choice. But she also observes that congregations offering teens a sense of belonging, a sense of meaning, and opportunities to grow those competencies are best able to keep them involved and engaged throughout their high school years.[24] This is just what we've been saying all along, and doing these things—creating belonging, developing opportunities for involvement, providing a sense of meaning—all need careful planning, leadership skills, and passion.

So just being a good guy or gal, being able to play the best basketball, or play the piano or guitar better than your students or church members, does not qualify you to coordinate ministry for young people. It takes a whole church of volunteers, parents, teachers, leaders, pastors, youth leaders, pre-teen teachers, music specialists, working all together to make it happen.

multiple intelligences and ministry

I would be remiss if I didn't talk about the power of multiple intelligences in light of good ministry to the young. This challenge highlights how important it is to build a cohesive team in working with your children and young people in your local congregation rather than focusing on the personality of one leader.

The concept of multiple intelligences provides for our guidance a research finding that can make a difference in your own ministry to young people, and in fact, to everyone in the church.

While this theory of learning is not new, it provides insight into how people learn and supports the *team theory* of ministry to young people. Dr. Howard Gardner, a professor of education at Harvard University articulated eight different intelligences to account for a broader range of human potential for young people and adults. These intelligences are:

(1) *Linguistic intelligence ("word smart");*
(2) *Logical-mathematical intelligence ("number/reasoning smart");*
(3) *Spatial intelligence ("picture smart"):*
(4) *Bodily-Kinesthetic intelligence ("body smart");*
(5) *Musical intelligence ("music smart");*
(6) *Interpersonal intelligence ("people smart");*
(7) *Intrapersonal intelligence ("self smart");*
(8) *Naturalistic intelligence ("nature smart").*

Most of the styles of learning fall into the categories of linguistic and logical-mathematical intelligence, but Dr. Gardner suggested that this theory, based on research, provides renewed insight into all of the ways people learn. This theory has implication for all types of learning, including faith development. Perhaps one of the most important features of his theory is how it can be applied to our ministry. He provided "eight different potential pathways" to learning. These give us some basic guidelines on how to apply this theory to our understanding of God and provides us with ideas as to how to develop our gifts to make them more effective in working with others. These pathways are:

() words (linguistic intelligence)

() numbers or logic (logical-mathematical intelligence)

() pictures (spatial intelligence)

() music (musical intelligence)

() self-reflection (intrapersonal intelligence)

() a physical experience (bodily-kinesthetic intelligence)

() a social experience (interpersonal intelligence, and/or

() an experience in the natural world. (naturalist intelligence)[25]

In religious instruction, these multiple intelligences are evident too. For example, we use ritual to touch the spatial and musical intelligences. The church uses sermons and teaching as a way at getting to linguistic and logical-mathematical intelligence. Or, for example, sports programs and outings in nature reach other intelligences. All these ways people learn demand competence and inclusion in all aspects of learning. Teaching people about God is equally complex as any other learning skill. Therefore, it is imperative that the church recognize that more people must be involved than simply a charismatic leader. Your ministry team can have gifts that nurture these multiple aspects of learning.

This sacred cow must be put to rest if we are going to be thorough and competent in our teaching and sharing of the magnificent experience of God in the world and in our lives. After all, no one person can do it all!

sacred cow no. 6: the best youth leaders are young and cool.

How would you describe the "ideal" youth or young adult leader? What do they look like and how do they act?

Often we think that a great young person's leader has to be somebody who is "cool" or someone who just knows about the latest fads and fashions. Should they be extroverted or introverted? Do they have to know how to play the guitar or the keyboard?

Do they have to have a great CD collection of new and unheard praise songs or be a Christian rock star? Of course, they have to be able to skateboard and text message, and probably they should be near the same age as their target ministry. Are "cool" well-dressed young people the only role models who can touch the youth of today? This sacred cow needs to be busted here and now.

qualities of a caring leader

We have already shared some qualities of both leaders and churches that make young people want to get involved in their congregational life—such things as demonstrating belonging and acceptance, providing identity opportunities, being grace-oriented in one's approach with young people. However, since much of youth and young adult ministry today requires models that are more complex and often relational, there is much more expected from the leader than in the past. It used to be that a frisbee, guitar and softball game might get you an audience that could listen to your sermon. Now, young people need to trust their leaders, be inspired and challenged by their own involvement in ministry, and provided with opportunity to become more than they are through association with mentors that truly care about them and what they believe and how they live.

A quotation in the Washington Post about the professionalizing of youth ministry says, "Even a decade ago, the model was 'Hey, if you're faithful and good with kids, hop on board.' More and more now, there is a realization that you need to be skilled to do this; it's not just hanging out with youth. It's being able to manage budgets, deal with parents—someone who can make this a living faith, not just something that's religious trivia."[26]

Actually, creating a job description for those who work with the young is not that difficult. Common sense rules here. Let's begin with the obvious.

try this. *Leader Qualities.* Use the space below to jot down a couple of things that would identify a quality leader for your own church's ministry to young people.

Quality #1: _____

Quality #2: _____

Quality #3: _____

Here is what my list of attributes necessary for working with your young people.

(1) *Loving Jesus and having a desire to share His love.*

(2) *Being a good listener about the world in which they live.*

(3) *Having an authenticity about your own journey of faith.* Young people have a way of knowing someone who is fake right away. And even if you can't text message, young people need others who are willing to be real with them about their own struggles and joys of faith life as a Christian. They can tell if you mean it.

(4) *Learning to love unconditionally.* This is a hard one. We usually love with a reason, for something. We are nice because being nice gets a good response. But loving as Jesus loved is a gift. Young people always need people in their lives who know how to care about them and who want to know them where they are and what they are truly like. And knowing this, they still feel loved.

(5) *All this means learning to have time for young people.* Everyone is very busy, and leaders are no different than anyone else. Because of this fact, recognize that youth are crying out for people who have time to just hang out.

(6) *Feeling comfortable building relationships and not being afraid to share your values and faith experience.* This does not mean just sharing what you believe and the doctrines that frame your understanding of God (theology). Rather, it means that even if you can do that, you feel free in sharing what God is doing now in your life. This faith-talk can be most constructive in opening doors to deeper relationships.

(7) *A willingness to learn about young people and explore new methods to reach out and become their friends.*

It is a proven fact that interest is more significant than age when working with other people. People that share the same interests often can relate better than people of the same age. A recent survey in *Group* magazine found that only nine percent of youth felt their youth leader should be young. This fact reemphasizes what is truly important.

Being "cool" and "flashy" may be fun, but certainly not needed to build effective ministry. In its place, substitute caring, concern, and intentional ministry that builds relationships. When that is done, involvement becomes natural. People want to be around people who accept and challenge them. This sacred cow is busted!

sacred cow no. 7: youth are so apathetic they will never get involved.

This sacred cow simply is not true. No one has more excitement and passion than young people. On the surface one might ask, If adolescents and Christianity are both so filled with passion, then why aren't young people flocking to the church?

There is no easy answer to this question. It may be so because the message given to young people about salvation is simply too ambiguous, the "call" to follow just too vague. Or, on the other hand, it may be because the "call" we give doesn't reflect the truth about God's actions in the one's life. What excites youth is natural passion and we must let that passion lead to deep faith and that faith move responsible people to action or ministry.[27] In our research about adolescence and faith development, over three-forths saw themselves committed to Jesus, and even more, some 93% "agreed somewhat" or "agreed very much" that they followed the teaching of their church. So claiming commitment to Jesus or a denomination does not seem to be the problem.

The gospel message is direct. God loves us, and because of this love he died for us. In some unique way, Jesus becomes a substitute for our often sinful lives and in the long run is acceptable to God in our place. That is the atonement doctrine simplified. What follows is a life of responsibility. This responsibility includes commitment to a new way, clearer decisions about life, and a set of values rooted in the nature of God Himself.

the passion of youth

Adolescence is by nature very passionate, according to the psychologist Erik Erikson. If the church does not capitalize on this developmental phenomenon, it misses its opportunity. What is the call of the church to these young people?

The calling of the disciples is an excellent illustration of the power of God's calling. Put yourself beside the Sea of Galilee in the first century. The environment is rural, with only a scattering of major cities within a day's walk of the seaside home of Jesus. Capernaum was a fishing village. The whole environment and vocation of its inhabitants was about the little lake. Jesus shows up and goes to the heart of their futures. They were used to fishing for fish, but Jesus' call to shift this to fishing for humans drew them out of their patterned lives and thrust them to think about larger possibilities. That is what the call of God does for people.

History is full of people that changed their lives because of commitment to a new life or challenge. This is what is central to the calling of God in the life. God comes to us in myriad ways, using various means to reach us. His coming brings new possibilities and new directions. With it comes a new set of values; in short, a brand new world view. His call of love, motivated through the grace of the Father, redirected their lives to think about something they had never considered.

Their lives were lived now following the passion of the new way. And in the same way, God comes to each of us and to our young people. It comes through the church, by way of leaders and mentors, or through the contact and relationships of their important friends.

So make sure your church challenges young people to be their best and to make good decisions about their life because Jesus made the ultimate choice to love and die in our place. The Gospel is a passionate motivator and resonates with the passion innate in each young person. Apathy is always short-lived in the presence of real change and deep commitment.

sacred cow no. 8: my church can never change.

The last sacred cow to eliminate repeats the adage that things just don't change. The church may be one institution that has a great many cultures, rich history, and grounded tradition attached to it. And making things happen in your church may seem like an impossibility. But, don't despair, there is help in the next generation.

Institutional change is always slow in contrast to individual change. Youth and young adult ministry is always in the process of change since youth basically have no history, or if they do, it is usually short. The church, on the other hand, brings to the table years of practice and ritual. The ageless music of the church is simply a part of their consciousness and reality. But for young people, their music memory always includes drums! Since their reality has little history, change always seem a possibility.

And therefore, keep in touch with your youth. See what trends are central to their lives. Check to see what models of ministry appeal to them. Chances are you will find that they always live near the edge of a tradition. So what is your challenge to get them involved in their own church?

(1) *Make ministry central.* Try to recommit your local church to the centrality of ministry for and with young people. That means everyone must learn to care. We don't want to lose our youth to the world, and so the church must become a safe place for them to abide. They must see a caring church.

(2) *Clarify the models.* Move your church to explore some of the models of ministry and methods of church that are compatible with the concerns of your youth. And at the same time, try to let the youth see the value in the "traditions" and "rituals" of the local congregation. They must see a relevant church.

(3) *Be ready for change.* Be ready for everyone to make some shift. Change is always a two-way street. As the youth adapt, the adults make some changes too. They must see an open church.

(4) *Find some common ground.* Not all of the likes and dislikes of the young are alien to the older members of your church. You will probably need to have some type of focus group or discussions together to resolve these tensions. A major problem in making change happen is that both sides don't talk to each other. They must see a church ready to dialogue.

(5) *Get everyone listening.* Get some of the thought leaders of the church together with some young people to listen to their desires about music, order of service, sermon topics, involvement of children, youth, and young adults in the service. Make sure you pick adults who know how to listen and don't bring their own agenda to the table. And then on the other side, pick youth that can articulate their wants and desires in a clear, non-threatening way. They must truly hear the church listening.

(6) *Make a few changes.* Give everyone a chance to suggest some changes in your church. Make sure everyone's represented, if possible. Then, make some change. Test the change out to see how it flies. Keep the discussion open and flowing as you institute some changes in your church. They all want to be represented.

have you killed any cows lately?

The story is told that some years ago right before the turn of the century, a young boy attended his first year of school in his native country, Germany. He had a high forehead, soulful eyes, and a shy smile. Usually the teacher overlooked him, but one day he surprised the young boy by calling him to the front of the class. The teacher held out his hand. On his palm were four coins. "Tell me the value of these coins," he asked. The boy looked up, stammered at first and then started. "Sir, you have a set with different sequences that have different values."

Astounded, the teacher looked at him and then shouted, "Dumkopf, what is the value of these coins?" The boy tried again. "Sir, you have a set with different sequences depending on the order, the values may differ."

"Dumkopf!" The teacher was outraged. "Do you think you are funny?" Without waiting for an answer he grabbed the boy by the shoulder and pulled him to a stool in the front of the class. The young boy finished the class in misery sitting on the stool facing the rest of the class with a tall yellow cap on his head and a sign pinned to his shirt saying 'Dumkopf'.

The young boy lived to a ripe old age. History has mercifully forgotten the teacher's name, but we'll never forget the author of 'E=MC^2', the young boy, Albert Einstein. (Einstein never did learn to make change!)

Now this may just be a good story, but it does share an important concept. We just don't know the potential within the young people of our church. History will only tell us the truth. Our challenge is to provide opportunity for each and every individual young person to strive to be what God wants them to be. The church is the place where this can happen. But only "if."

If the church takes seriously the centrality and importance of ministry to these challenging age groups.

If the leaders take seriously the value of each young person who is trying to become more than they are.

If the membership of the local church sheds its presuppositions about what young people should be like and learns to accept them as they come, and as they are.

If you and I recommit ourselves to being the types of people that can mentor the faith of others because we have recommitted ourselves to the gospel of Jesus Christ.

chapter 3 / endnotes

1. Tim Neufeld, "Postmodern Models of Youth Ministry," *Direction* (Fall 2002, Vol. 31. No. 2.) 194-205.

2. Kennon Callahan, *Effective Church Leadership: Building on the Twelve Keys* (New York, NY: Harper & Row, 1990), 19-20.

3. Tony Jones, *Postmodern Youth Ministry: Exploring Cultural Shift, Creating Holistic Connections, Cultivating Authentic Community* (Grand Rapids, MI: Zondervan, 2001), 24-17.

4. Leonard I. Sweet, *Soul Tsunami* (Grand Rapids, MI: Zondervan, 1999), 215-222.

5. See Doug Fields, *Purpose Driven Youth Ministry: Nine Essential Foundations for Healthy Growth* (Grand Rapids, MI: Zondervan, 1998).

6. See Doug Fields, *Purpose Driven Youth Ministry and Duffy Robbins, Ministry of Nurture, (Grand Rapids, MI: Zondervans,* 1990).

7. See Jim Burns, *Youth Builder: Today's Resource for Relational Youth Ministry* (Ventura, CA: Gospel Light Publications, 2002).

8. This is the most traditional model of ministry for young people. Its two-pronged strategy provides activities for church youth and encourages them to reach out to others. While it had its beginnings in the 1930s and '40s, it still provides a valid approach for small congregations with limited resources.

9. See Tom Zanzig, "Youth Ministry: Reflections and Directions" *Readings and Resources in Youth Ministry*, ed. by Michael Warren (Winona, WI: St. Mary's Press, 1987).

10. This model was identified and labeled by the Churches Youth Ministry Association in New Zealand. On their website: http://www.youthministry.org. nz/?sid=42&id-20 accessed on 11/2/06 you can see this model clarified in five settings (1. Youth Programming, 2. Family Ministry, 3. Faith Community, 4. School Community, 5. Local Community); using two methods (1. Gathered programs and, 2. Non-gathered programs); and utilizing eight separate components (1. Advocacy, 2. Catechism/Religious Education, 3. Community Life, 4. Evangelism, 5. Guidance & Counselling or Pastoral Care, 6. Justice, Peace and Service, 7. Leadership Development and 8. Prayer and Worship).

11. There are myriad models of young people's ministry that have been created and explored. Many of the themes in one type are duplicated in one of another name. Here are some websites that might be helpful in look-

ing at the various models of youth ministry extant. Below are some links to sites describing a myriad of models of youth ministry: <http://batteriesnotincluded.digitalorthodoxy.com/?page_id=11>is a paper which describes philosophical models of youth ministry, including church-centered, society-centered, and middle ground. This article also links to more articles on models of youth ministry. <http://members.aol.com/mleslie598/teams.htm> is a site with an excellent overview of team ministry in youth ministry, and includes samples of different roles that can be taken within a team ministry. <http://www.sonlifeafrica.com/model/main.htm> is a site dedicated to the Son Life model of youth ministry. This site has lots of useful information beyond just looking at the Son Life model as well, including articles for youth ministers, program ideas, articles about youth, and more! <http://www.directionjournal.org/article/?1265> is an article describing four models of "postmodern" youth ministry taken from Mark Senter's Four Views of Youth Ministry and the Church (2001, Zondervan: Grand Rapids) . These four models are based on the idea of fellowship and mission. <http://www.tomorrowtoday;.biz/mindthegap/thesishonours/ch4.htm> is a section of Graeme Codrington's thesis detailing his Spiritual Growth model of youth ministry.

12. Mark H. Senter III, (ed), Wesley Black, Chap Clark, Malan Nel, *Four Views of Youth Ministry and the Church* (Grand Rapids, MI: Zondervans, 2001), 23-38.
13. Mark H. Senter III, *Four Views of Youth Ministry and the Church,* 39-76.
14. Mark H. Senter III, *Four Views of Youth Ministry and the Church,* 77-112.
15. Mark H. Senter III, *Four Views of Youth Ministry and the Church,* 113-152.
16. Tim Neufeld, "Postmodern Models of Youth Ministry," 3.
17. Norman Herr, *The Sourcebook for Teaching Science: Strategies, Activities and Internet Resources,* accessed on 11/7/06 at <http://www.csun.edu/science/health/docs/tv&health.html>, 1.
18. Norman Herr, *The Sourcebook for Teaching Science,* 2.
19. Jim Burns, Mike DeVries, *The Youth Builder* (Ventura, CA: Gospel Light, 2001), 109.
20. Jim Burns, *The Youth Builder,* 110.
21. For a complete discussion about the age-referents for conversion experience as an identity function, see, V. Bailey Gillespie, *The Dynamics of Religious Conversion,* (Birmingham, AL: Religious Education Press, 1991), 95-109.
22. Chap Clark, Kara E. Powell, Deep *Ministry in a Shallow World* (Zondervans, 2006), 155.
23. Visit a view of his model of commitment at <http://www.sonlifeafrica.com/model/index.htm>. Assessed on 11/7/06.
24. See Carol E. Lytch, *Choosing Church: What Makes a Difference for Teens* (Louisville, KY: Westminster John Knox Press, 2004).
25. For a detailed description of how the multiple intelligences impact teaching in all areas of learning, see: Thomas Armstrong, *Multiple Intelligences in the Classroom* (Alexandria, VA: Association of Supervision and Curriculum Developmemnt, 1994) and Howard Gardner, *Frames of Mind: The Theory of Multiple Intelligences* (New York, NY: Basic Books, 1983) and *Multiple Intelligences: The Theory in Practice* (New York, NY: Basic Books, 1993).
26. Quoted in the article entitled, "Ministering with New Maturity: Good with kids isn't enough in youth posts," in the *Washington Post* on Sunday, August 6, 2006; page C01.
27. Probably the best discussion of young people and their passionate committment to God can be found in Kendra Creasy Dean, *Practicing Passion:Youth and the Quest for a Passionate Church* (Grand Rapids, MI: Eerdmans, 2004).

chapter 4

getting involved in your local church

before we get specific about the various ways to involve young people in local church life, we want to lay out some basic principles that can help your church. These principles can enrich the quality of ministry to young people as well as provide you with some practical ideas that illustrate the principles disclosed here.

These principles are foundational in providing some rationale for ministry. But first, let me share a true story.

Every weekend someone's looking for the youth pastor. He's involved in everything in the church and in the ministry for its young people. That ministry can be really tough and yet rewarding at the same time. The youth pastor in this story has way too many responsibilities. There is not enough time to get everything done, so something suffers. The demands on the youth or young adult professional in local settings is enormous. Most pastors can't simply specialize in youth or young adult ministry. Their responsibilities lie somewhere between Jack of all trades and miracle worker. If the job is to minister to everyone, someone loses. If it is not the ministry itself, it's often the youth pastor's family that suffers.

Now, if you don't have a youth or young adult specialist at your church, then this chapter is still for you—adult leaders— you can be guilty of the same over-reaching and energy-depleting schedules.

But even with this scenario played out on a weekly basis for many professionals in ministry, the same is true for lay workers. Their jobs are always coupled with their desire to do ministry and family, and they face the same challenges. So the first principle is basic. Ministry to children, preteens, youth, and young adults, is a team effort.

principle no. 1: you can not do it alone; you will need help

In reality, everyone in the church is a youth or young adult pastor. Yes, that is right. Take a look at your local church. How many people do you have involved in the ministry of the adult population in your congregation? There are elders, deacons, deaconesses, religious education superintendents, ushers, a welcome team of couples, community service groups, finance committee members, choir members, treasurers, teachers, childrens' leaders, youth leaders, and perhaps even a young adult coordinator. The majority of adults involved in ministry may be a bit lopsided. Emphasis on adult religious education and ministry is often what takes precedence over those smaller divisions and age-related groups in the church.

If your church or Christian school wants to get young people involved, you must find the able bodied people that can build a ministry team in the same proportions that you have as you minister to the adult population. Why? Well, that is simple. Since feeling like they belong is a developmental task that can be met by active caring and providing a sense of importance for the young, any church that wants to be in the forefront of ministry to young people must make it a priority to build a balanced team in all areas of young people's ministry. It is everyone's problem and challenge at the same time.

It is important to understand that one of the methods God uses to get his message out to the world is that of individuals working together. The church is a community of individuals committed to a central cause. Dietrich Bonhoeffer, in *Life Together* said, "In a Christian community everything depends upon whether each individual is an indispensable link in a chain. Only when even the smallest link is securely interlocked is the chain unbreakable

. . .It will be well, therefore, if every member receives a definite task to perform for the community, that he may know in hours of doubt that he, too, is not useless and unusable."[1]

That means that every pastor is a young person's pastor. Every teacher, even adult leader, and yes, every member is a pastor too. Every elder, deacon, treasurer, and so on is to see young people's ministry as a central part of their own job description. Together they work as a team. Spread the work, spread the blame, and spread the love around.

principle no. 2: do something, anything!

Let's begin with some new and interesting research facts about pre-teen, youth, and young adult ministry in the local church. We'll see if we can derive some more principles that can be applied to the church in general and to ministry to the young in particular, and you'll see that churches can't afford to sit back and do nothing regarding these vital ministries.

When we review the research we have conducted with young people, we learn some interesting facts about ministry. Here is a summary of our research findings in this area. These conclusions reflect the research the Hancock Center for Youth and Family Ministry has been is involved in over the past 20 years.

valuegenesis research summarized[2]: why ministry to the young people in your church is so crucial.

() Any exposure to and involvement in youth ministry has a positive impact on young people's relationship to the church and its major doctrines and beliefs.

() As young people are exposed to more ministry, youth have higher levels of commitment to these same beliefs and values.

() When young people are exposed to higher levels to and involvement in youth ministry, they develop a higher degree of intrinsic orientation to religion, which in turn leads to higher levels of intention for future involvement in the church.

() As you would expect, faith maturity is higher among young people who have had higher levels of exposure to and involvement in youth ministry.

() Young people have less involvement in "at-risk" behaviors and are protected from the dangers of these behaviors. Surrounding youth with positive peers helps in this process.[3]

() Young people involved in church ministry have less depression and are also less likely to think about suicide.

() Ministry to the young is imperative if we want to have young people be loyal to their church.

() Church pastors are perceived as having greater influence in youth's lives when ministry to them is a serious element of their church's life.

() When young people are involved in church and its ministry programming, they see the church as more exciting, warm, friendly, and inviting.

() When youth lead out in worship they tend to own the church and see it as much more relevant.

As you can see, our research shows the close relationship with how young people view and think about their church as well as how they feel about its central teachings and behaviors. Barry Gane, youth specialist says, "The general results tell us that if our only goal was to produce young adults who give mental assent to the doctrinal position of the church, then we are having reasonable success. . . . Just like their counterparts in society at large, they will not give loyalty to an organization just because their parents are part of it. Although respect for pastoral leadership is not automatically given, youth ministry enhances the chances that they will both connect with and respect their pastors."[4]

Other research supports these *Valuegenesis* findings as well. Christian Smith and Melinda Denton have conducted a comprehensive and reliable project providing insight into the relationship of religions in the lives of cross-generational young people. They surveyed 3000 teens (aged 13-17) and their parents. Written surveys were complemented by 267 face-to-face interviews of teens in 45 states. Their research is often touted as better than the two other major quantitative researchers in this field, George Barna and George Gallup. What did they find? Here is a summary of some of the research findings that relate to this American teenagers and their search for religious and spiritual lives.

more research[5]: regarding the religious and spiritual lives of american teenagers

() This study confirms that parents are the key influences for teen's religious lives. Three out of four religious teens consider their own beliefs somewhat or very similar to their parents. (Three out of four say they are more similar to their mothers' beliefs than to their fathers').

() Peers may be important to teens, but parents are still the primary influence in religion.

() Teenagers are not a "people apart, or an alien race about whom adults can only shake their heads and look forward to their growing up."

() "Any generation gap that exists between teens and adults today is superficial compared with and far outweighed by the generational commonalities." Simply stated, it implies that way too much has been make of the differences between Generation X, Generation Y, the millennial generation, the lost generation, baby busters, the 13th generation, etc.

() Youth don't seem to be flocking to alternative religions and spiritualities. Most teens identify themselves as Christians.

() Over half of these teens said religion was important to their lives and only 8% suggested it was not important at all.

() They saw their congregations as warm and welcoming.

() 75% saw themselves a part of the same kind of congregation at age 25. Our *Valuegenesis* research claims 72% saw themselves a part of the same denomination at age 40.

() Teens are traditional. "Contrary to popular perceptions, the vast majority of American adolescents are not spiritual seekers or questers of the type often described by journalists and some scholars, but are instead mostly oriented toward and engaged in conventional religious traditions and communities. Teens seem to be both spiritual and denominationally located."

() Teens in the general public in America seem to believe in a type of "Moralistic Therapeutic Deism," a middle way between organizational religion and individual religion that is idiosyncratic, eclectic, and syncretistic.

() And finally, most teen problems are linked to adult problems.

The more people you involve in ministry the higher will be the perception of ministry to your youth. The more you do, the better the results. It's a simple logical deduction. More ministry, more involvement, more commitment, more loyalty. All a church has to do is commit to make young people a key evangelistic and nurture target for the church. Often churches are so involved in bringing people with no connection to the church that they neglect those that are already there. Nurture is not an ugly word. Nurture implies caring for those in the fold. Build a team and get working together. This deserves a couple of speeches in a church board meeting; right?

As you can see, both parents and the church itself are crucial in the ministry of the young. Let's move to a discussion about the role of the church in this task. The church represents Christ, according to the New Testament. The church is Christ's representative organization on this earth to mold and model the Kingdom. If the church doesn't represent Christ in His fullness, we will be facing an uphill battle in the faith growth of the young in our care. Principle number three explores just how to guarantee the faith of young people in your church.

principle no. 3: the church guarantees faith and the kingdom of god

The term, "Faith Guarantor" is a phrase I have used many times before and first encountered in graduate school when my major professor, a faith development expert, signed in his first book a message to me. It said, "For Bailey Gillespie—guarantor for youth."[6] It was the pop-cultural phrase among religious educators in the 1970s, but its meaning is still relevant today. It answers the question, "What is the role of the people of faith in the life of the church as it ministers to the world?"

The answer is obvious: *it guarantees what faith is all about to every constituency in its purview.*

Erik Erikson, the distinguished psychoanalyst and historian, first introduced a concept close to this in his seminal work, *Young Man Luther.*[7] The reference in Erikson's work is to Father Staupitz, head of the Augustinian Order of which Martin Luther was a student. It seems that Father Staupitz was the person who stood by

Luther to affirm and counsel him during his emotional and theological crisis.[8]

Ross Snyder, a Christian religious educator applied it to youth ministry when he said, "Being a Guarantor assumes of the leader a warmth, authenticity, and healthy outlook on life, a spirit of optimism and confidence in the future, and requires of him or her a living with youth that inspires respect, trust, and communication. It is the leader as Guarantor, able to bridge the generation gap with discerning and affirming presence, who gives assurance to a youth and guarantees, as it were, that he or she can successfully cope with the business of growing up and can eventually 'make it.'"[9]

The church is a guarantor. Parents are guarantors. Religious educators are guarantors too. Your ministry team are all guarantors of faith. Pastors and youth pastors guarantee faith. And you are a guarantor. Even if your only interface with youth is that of church member, you too are a guarantor of what faith is all about.

The power of others is significant in mentoring faith. Resiliency research helps us here. For example, we know that if you want to help young people learn values and stay away from at-risk behaviors, then what is important is that they "hook-up" with someone that has clear values. Over time, say two to three years or more, the power of good seems to prevail and this relationship helps the young person to become bulletproof. That is the power of a guarantor.

In religion the target is not just values, but faith—a trusting relationship with God.

principle no. 4: your life has to be right with god

If you and God have not begun a close relationship, then this principle is for you. To be a guarantor of faith, one must be on the journey with God. This journey is just like any other one we decide to take. Sometimes things don't go all that well. At times we choose to get off the path or go a different direction altogether, but over the long haul, your walk with God grows and your commitment strengthens. If not, you will burn out doing ministry or simply lose interest in what is important to God.

Doug Fields, basing his approach on a Purpose Driven Ministry, shares a number of key attitudes you can develop that can help you set a healthy pace for your ministry to teens. These attributes need to be cultivated in each of those who lead, direct, or interface with young people in local congregations. His suggestions provide a start in our renewal and refocus for our spiritual path. They describe areas of interface with young people in personal evaluation.

your spiritual check list: Use this check list to identify areas where you could do better. Check the areas where you could grow or improve.
- ❏ Guard your alone time with God
- ❏ Evaluate your commitment
- ❏ Try new things in your ministry to teens
- ❏ Treat humility as the key to ministry impact
- ❏ Don't be afraid to grow old
- ❏ Be an avid learner
- ❏ Glean wisdom from others[10]

If you want young people to become involved in your church, it is imperative that the lives of the leaders be truly an example. Peers always are important to young people, heros from sports or the movies are society's ways of fulfilling this personal need for examples and leadership. How much better if the leaders of ministry in a local church would exemplify the spiritual life. These mentors would make being religious during times when personal things don't seem to be working very well much easier.

The power of others can never be diminished. If a church wants young people involved, they have to model acceptance and openness. The warmth in the church must be contagious. The acceptance of young people must be real.

principle no. 5: getting youth involved is an intentional activity for any church

Nothing happens by chance. There are always reasons. Even when the learning is not planned, people still learn by default. That is why anything Christians do in ministry must be planned, prayed about, and acted on. Ministry is an intentional activity. Nothing happens unless we make a decision and do it.

Getting young people active in a local church does not happen without some thought and preparation. Being intentional simply means someone has made a conscious choice to do something. We've mentioned this concept briefly in an earlier chapter, but now we want to give it arms and legs, so to speak.

Here are some steps and activities that move your church to a planned course of action with young people with a goal of getting them involved in church and the religious life.

1. *Propose a mission, objectives or goals for your local ministry.* It all begins here. Nothing happens if you don't have a target. Take some time to create with your core group of young people a clear, brief statement of your purpose. This purpose statement is often called a Mission Statement.

try this. *Write a one sentence* (25 words or less) statement that completes the following statement: *"It is the purpose of our ministry to young people (youth ministry/children's ministry, etc.) to . . ."*

_____

_____

_____

_____

After careful thinking about your church's mission and purpose, move to the next step.

2. *Do a needs assessment.* Find out what your young people think. Ask them to give you some idea as to just what they think they want and need. Good planning always includes the "stakeholders" in any decisions. So don't forget to ask the people who receive ministry what they want. And you can include parents in this discussion, church leaders, pastors, as well as young people in your home-grown focus group.

Remember to poll every young person and not just a few. You don't want to make decisions about ministry without asking the opinions of those who receive. And if you can find people currently not involved, ask them too. It is the youth who seldom come that need ministry as well.

When you do assessments or evaluations, encourage honest responses. Find a time that is convenient for everyone. Do it when it is not an intrusion into the lives of your members, but let people know you value their honest and frank appraisal of the future of their ministry. Make sure that your assessment is focused and you communicate that you want to use the information to do things better.

You may want to do the following exercise to see just how your young people feel about your church's ministry.

try this. Here is an *evaluation activity* you can use to involve your young people in clarifying their choices. Get a bunch of small (lunch-bag size) paper sacks. Write on each bag a possible quality or statement about your proposed ministry. Here are some examples.

"My opinion counts here."

"I feel comfortable bringing my friends."

"This group is run by adults."

"I feel welcome in this group."

"I feel needed by this church."

"This church congregation cares about teens."

"If our leader were to leave, this group would fall apart."

"This group cares about me."

"I've felt closer to God through this group."

"I want to deal with issues that are important to me."

"We need more adults at our activities."

"Bible studies."

"How about retreats."

"I wish there was a youth choir."

"I want weekly meetings."

"Trips."

"Prayer."

"Worship.."

"Discussions."

"More games."

Tape or tack the sacks, open side up, to a wall. Give each a stack of green and red slips of paper. (These can be cut to about 1"X3" from construction paper.) Red and green index cards can also be used. Ask the young people to wander past the row of stacks on the wall. If they agree with a statement on a stack, they should drop in a green slip. If they disagree, drop in a red one. In sacks labeled with activities such as "Bible studies" and "Retreats" kids should deposit green slips if they feel these functions have been helpful; red slips if they have not been. Then divide the full bags, add votes and mark the result on the outside of the sacks. [11]

There are many ways to do a needs assessment. It can be done as informally as after a basketball game, or over pizza. It can be done casually after a meeting, or talking on the parking lot. Any way you do it is helpful. And don't forget the parents.

When we understand what our young people want, it is easier to balance that desire with what you know they may need to function in the real world as genuine Christians. Help them by involving them in making clear decisions about what is central to your church's mission. And don't forget to spend time in prayer and planning; it helps the church move to action.

3. *Propose a functional framework for youth ministry* After you see your purpose and have some sense about where your young people are, try to summarize their needs, your wants, and your purpose into a brief four or five part outline such as: Nurture, Education, Fellowship, Evangelism, and Service. Here is an activity you can do with your young people's group after you have created your ministry mission statement and clarified individual needs.

try this. *Balanced ministry.* On the right is a list of some things that might be included in a balanced ministry to the young. Give out the list to your ministry team or young people and ask them to select only four things that you could target as foci during the next year of ministry in your church. Then write the four you have chosen in the blanks on the left. There is room to add your own targets too.

My Ministry Targets	Possible Targets
1. _____	Evangelism
	Community Service
2. _____	Doctrinal Studies
	Fellowship
3. _____	Action
	Worship
4. _____	World Missions
	Grace
	Sharing
	Education
	Missions
	Church Involvement
	Personal Spiritual Life
	Bible understanding

There are many formulas that work. You might want to use Grace, Worship, Community, and Service; or how about Study, Sharing, Action, Fellowship as models of an organizational nature that outlines the various parts of your ministry.

Over the years in training sessions with youth professionals and children's ministers, I have noticed that regardless of what people say they want, coupled with what you, as a concerned parent or youth professional think they need, there are just so many categories that clarify most purposes of ministry to the young and you probably will identify most in four or five basic concepts.

4. *Develop a master calendar for your church.* How can your church plan anything for young people if they don't know what is already planned for them? Before you build a master calendar, check the school year, both public and church schools, the church calendar, holidays, and try to figure out your church's vacation schedule.

If you want to involve young people in your church, you have to understand their personal schedules and the things that impact their lives before you can begin to schedule events, activities, outings, and programming that is both effective and possible.

5. *Start planning being true to your purpose and objectives.* Now move to action. It is imperative that those who build youth and young adult ministries in local churches use a clear, mission-oriented approach to planning objectives and implementation. The time now is to move ahead. Make plans, build important communication—that means learning how to text message—and begin to transfer responsibility to the youth of your church. Responsibility builds ownership, ownership builds commitment and action.

6. *When it's over, do an evaluation and begin again.* Assessment is never done, according to those who know. Educators say that if it is not evaluated, it did not happen, so it is important to see if what you decided to do made any difference. Assessment is a big thing in contemporary businesses and schools, but is all too often forgotten by those in religious communities. So don't be remiss by not taking time to debrief, explore meaning, and make appropriate adjustments and changes. And then, start the cycle over again. Use the following assessment to see just how you are doing and what is important to the young people in your ministry.

try this. *Grade Report. Remember, nothing really happens if you can't evaluate it. So use this form to see how you are doing and what you might like to do next. Create this evaluation just like a grade card for school.* (A = Great; B = Good; C = OK; D = Not quite; F = You missed the mark).

Instructions: Give a grade to the following events, programs, and activities of our youth (young adult) ministry.

Description	Grade
1. Prayer groups	_____
2. Retreat "Share the Power"	_____
3. Youth choir	_____
4. Weekend worship	_____
5. Youth church	_____
6. Pastor's talks	_____
7. Bible studies	_____
8. Service project (community help week)	_____
9. Trips (Sea World)	_____
10. Lock-in	_____

The results of any survey process should give you many new ideas for new and creative directions for your ministry. Look carefully at the results. If your ministry does not seem to be effective, continue praying and asking God's direction, and in addition, check to see if you are meeting the needs of your local young people. Ministry to young people addresses the needs they have in a powerful and experiential way. What we want is a long-term, stable ministry that grows and is sufficient to function without your leadership.

So get everyone talking together and you'll find that your ministry will begin to be more effective and relevant.

principle no. 6: the best religious education takes place when youth are engaged in action learning

We conclude this chapter with an important principle for anyone working with young people. It is a word about methods. If you want young people to be involved in anything, you have to do three things:

1. Engage them in something that interests them (focus)
2. Give them real responsibility (ownership)
3. Wrap the approach in exciting energy (action)

Action learning is a method educators have become expert in for the classroom. Church educators, pastors, parent/leaders usually have not thought in terms of the types of methods that could be used to explore the wonders of Christian life.

The term "action learning" has been defined in a number of ways, but for our purposes, I'll use the following definition. "Action learning can be defined as a process in which a group of people come together more or less regularly to help each other learn from their experience."[12] Simply put, this method is particularly effective in church-related learning because it draws learning from experience. It is inductive in that regard because the principles of life are drawn from the experience of living. The experience can be just something that is happening.

There is a learning loop that is followed. It is cyclic. For example, all become involved in action; all reflect on that action. Consider the following simple learning cycle. This diagram captures the essence of the main features of experiential learning. At its simplest, it has two stages: Action and Reflection.

[action ☛ reflection]

However, after a series of cycles, the reflection seems to gain its point by leading to learning, which in turn leads to changes in behavior and belief in the future.[13]

[action ☛ reflection ☛ action ☛ planning ☛ action ☛ learning]

This theory of learning is based on the assumption that we can only make sense of our world in ways which build on our prior understanding. In enhancing that understanding by reflection of the experience, we become better able to act positively in the world. As you can see this theory of learning has important implications for faith development.

Jesus used this model throughout his ministry. He traveled throughout Israel stopping at villages. These events are, in a nutshell, the story of the ministry of Jesus: He did not have a grand plan of action, using the newspapers, media, propaganda, or meetings with huge crowds. Mostly, his plan of action was "one-on-one," with humble personal encounters.

These personal encounters with the Samaritan woman, or the Nobleman, or the leper, or the blind Bartimaeus, or the fisherman Peter, or the tax collector Matthew, or with Zacchaeus, or the widow of Nain, or the mother of Tyre healing her epileptic daughter, or with Nicodemus, or the thieves at the Cross—in just these little personal encounters He elucidates so many examples of life, theology, and philosophy that million of library book shelves all over the world are full of comments to his apparently simple remarks. His actions taught his message. This is action learning at its best.

With teens, like with all learners of any age, the action you are involved in informs your reflection and is informed by it, as well. The reflection produces the learning. Action is then changed as a result of the actual learning and leads to more learning and behavior changes. It models the actual way we grow and should be incorporated into almost every religious learning experience you provide for your young people.

This method is especially useful for youth. They learn most through actual experience. Review your ministry programs, sermons, activities, parties, and mission activities. See how much we use action to get our point across. However, this model, should we subscribe exclusively to it, requires some reflection, discussion, feedback on the activity . This debriefing is crucial if any learning and then change is to occur.

Examine the children's programs in your church. Notice that children never sit still. They use felt boards, sticks, musical instruments, walking, jumping, singing, movement all to teach basic religious principles. But around the 6th grade, somehow we stop most of the action and expect young people to sit quietly and listen to some adult propose their way of life. Sadly, most young people go through some forgetting of religion between the junior high and senior high years because of this transition in method.

try this. *Action Object Lessons.* If you need an activity at the last minute, try giving to five of your youth the following objects: (brick, balloon, needle, toy animal, pillow). Ask these recipients to go to another room and spend 10 minutes preparing a 5-minute talk (sermon) using this object as an illustration of the religious life or God's actions in this world. When they return, watch the group listen and think about what each object reminds them of in their own Christian life.

Action heightens attention, and a keen, attentive mind can focus and clarify important issues. Action learning is a crucial tool in building involvement and commitment.

Wayne French in his book *Creating Memories for Teens* suggests, "To teach His lessons, God used as many senses as possible. This meant that the principles being taught would long be remembered. Nothing in the Bible was to be accepted blindly. He wanted people to be able to think through the events, to have their own ideas and concepts, and to be able to truly learn the meaning of those events in their own lives."[14]

In the Bible, action learning is central. Through the use of narrative and story, God's people are seen in their struggles, victories, challenges, and disappointments. In actions, God is understood—the pillar of fire, the cloud of covering, the opening of the sea, the story of Job, the actions of the growing New Testament church.

All of God's communication in the Bible is set in story form. Without the action of the stories, the truths would not be made as clear as they are due to the demonstrative, action-filled lives of the people of God.

try this. *Bible Action Stories.* Here are some stories you can use as you illustrate specific Bible truths. When you tell the story, note the actions, the interactions, and the drama that helps get the point across. After telling the story, ask (debrief) what the purpose of the story was, and what we could learn about God's concern for us through the story line. *(We've provided some help to direct your thinking about the purpose of these stories.)*

○ Matthew 8:23-27 (Calming of the Sea) — All about trust
○ 1 Samuel 3 (Young Samuel) — Hearing God is important
○ Jeremiah 35:1-15 (Obedient people) — Hearing and doing is crucial
○ Daniel 1 (Daniel's health challenge) — God cares about you
○ Luke 19 (Zacchaeus the tax man) — Sinners can respond
○ Philemon (Onesimus and Paul) — Partners care for others

We hope you can take the principles in this chapter, couple them with the research we've explored, and move your church's ministries for the young to new levels of involvement. Take what you can, redo it, try it, try it again, but in the end, do something that engages young people and challenges them to love of Jesus.

chapter 4 / endnotes

1. Dietrich Bonhoeffer, *Life Together* (San Francisco, CA: Harper & Row, 1954), 94.

2. Our thanks to the research team that put together the *Valuegenesis* research study looking at faith, values, and commitment in the lives of Seventh-day Adventist young people over the first ten-year period of research. Its findings are found in V.. Bailey Gillespie, Michael J. Donahue with Ed Boyatt and Barry Gane, *Ten Years Later: A Study of Two Generations* (Lincoln, NE: AdventSource, 2004). A copy can be purchased [On line] at www.hancockcenterstore.com. These youth ministry specific findings can be found explored in detail in Barry Gane, *Youth Ministry and Beliefs and Values among 10-19-year-old students in the Seventh-day Adventist School System in North America*. A dissertation for the degree of Ph.D., Andrews University, 2005. 155-160. They have been summarized here. Dr. Gane is on the research team for the *Valuegenesis* project for the North American Division of Seventh-day Adventists.

3. At-risk behaviors include, alcohol use, drug use, tobacco use, shoplifting, depression, getting in trouble in school, violence in school, eating disorders, binge drinking, sex, and suicide.

4. Barry Gane, *Youth Ministry Beliefs and Values*, 157-158.

5. See Christian Smith, with Melinda Denton, *Soul Searching: The Religious and Spiritual Lives of American Teenagers* (New York, NY: Oxford University Press, 2005).

6. Paul B. Irwin, *The Care and Counseling of Youth in the Church* (Philadelphia, PA: Fortress Press, 1975), i.

7. Erik Erikson, *Young Man Luther,* (New York, NY: W.W. Norton & Co., 1958), 17, 37, 147, 156.

8. Paul B. Irwin, *Care and Counseling*, 3.

9. Ross Snyder, "The Ministry of Meaning" in *Risk* (Geneva, Switzerland: Youth Department of the World Council of Churches and World Council of Christian Education). 1 (1965), 137-143. The concept, "Guarantor of Faith" was in paganism attributed to the god Mithra. In the time of the early church, the Holy Spirit was ascribed this function.

10. From *Group Magazine Features* [On line]. Available at <http://www.group-mag.com/current/Feature1106asp>, accessed on 11/8/06.

11. Thom Shultz, Joani Schultz, *Involving Youth in Youth Ministry* (Loveland, CO: Group Books, 1987), 33-35.

12. Bob Dick, (1997) *Action Learning and Action Research* [On line]. Available at <http://www.scu.edu.au/schools/gcm/ar/arp/actlearn.html>. 1-2.

13. Bob Dick, (1997) *Action Learning*, 3-4.

14. Wayne French, *Creating Memories for Teens* (Warburton, Victoria: Signs Publishing Company, 2005), 24. There is a particularly good chapter that provides biblical examples of action learning. See pages 21-27.

chapter 5

getting involved
in spiritual life

You hear a lot these days about being spiritual. Research about teens often points to a dichotomy between the spiritual life and the religious life. We have even made the statement that teens in our *Valuegenesis* research project seem to be "more spiritual and less religious." But before you jump to any conclusions or observations yourself about this and your church teens, statements like that need some clarification as well as some definitional understanding.

Usually, we contrast being "religious" and "spiritual" by placing them on a continuum. On the one side is religious and on the other, a long way apart, is the term spiritual. This contrast may be too extreme. The bumper sticker theology, "After Religion Try Jesus," is way too simple an explanation of the actual situation.

For example, for most, being "spiritual" has to do with personal, vertical religious life—such things as prayer, spiritual vocations, meditation, deep Bible study, reflection and devotion.

"Religious," on the other hand, is usually defined in organizational terms and describes primary commitment to organized religious life—church attendance, denominational loyalty, church affiliation—along with over commitment to what some might disparagingly call, "The kingdom of God industry."

Ken Curtis, a former student and now pastor said it this way after attending a project on Boomers and Busters at a mountain retreat: "Our first major discovery, the common thread that ran through the unique needs and perspectives of boomers, busters, and the pastors who had gathered to study them, was their deep hunger for genuine spirituality. All three groups had become weary of how kingdom life had been replaced by the kingdom of God industry; how marketing had replaced caring; how production had replaced significance; and how knowing Jesus had become one item to select on a divine smorgasbord of options, rather than the central core from which everything else flowed. We, of course, knew better. Given a test, we would have earned passing scores. But that was not the way it was typically being lived out in the actual practice of boomers, busters or pastors."[1]

The church organization at its best is a reflection of the spiritual life. Prayer, Bible study, devotions and the like can flow from a community, deeply organized and committed to life together, reflecting these commitments and organizing themselves around a calling that comes from clear responses based on reflection of what is perceived as the will of God. That is the best scenario.

Of course, we often see church organizations at their worst. Many suffer from human passions and flaws. After all, they are human organizations. The early church had their problems, the disciples had their misunderstandings, and we are no different. And if you contrast the spiritual life with a "bad" or "dysfunctional" organization, the continuum contrasts are clear. But if you describe the church as a community of common concern, a family with Christ as the head, a group of people seeking God's will, founded on prayer and study, along with compassion, then you have a close relationship with that of the spiritual life.

One might argue that when we have a close walk with God, deepened through community and responsibility, fashioned through the process of reflection on God's will in Scripture, and relevant in the real world because of its involvement in its challenges and responsive because of its care, we see a close relationship between being spiritual people and religious church members.

the role of parents and church members

Where does it all begin? Before we talk specifically about young people and what the church can do to help them get involved on the personal level, we would be remiss without mentioning again the power of parents and a Christ-filled home, and by extension, the power of adult mentors in creating a church that is positive and inviting for young people.

It is important to spend time in your local church teaching parents and other church members how to reflect quality in the style and approach to young people, perhaps starting some focus groups or discussions with parents using professional counselors who can assist in providing suggestions as to how to build confidence in parents and members alike. Or the church itself could plan parenting ministries that would refocus the whole church on the need for including young people in the spiritual life of the church as well as the organizational aspect of ministry to others.

share this. *Church/Family Goals.* Clarifying your goals as a church regarding your ministry to the young is an important first step. Here is a list of qualities that some church members believe would be helpful targets regarding spiritual life and the church's relationship to it.

1. Assist in developing a close, personal friendship with Jesus.
2. Teach growing young Christians to filter life through a Christian worldview.
3. Deepen knowledge of God's word and understanding of its truths.
4. Encourage the application of biblical insights into daily living.
5. Share Christ through life, work, service and witness.
6. Instill a faith that can function in daily life apart from the church and family.[2]

These qualities encompass the spiritual goals a church might have for its young. Couple this with good Christian parenting, and you have completed the first step in building personal piety and fellowship with Christ into your church or family life. Teens have some concerns about their parents too. They would like to see quality parenting at home. If the church builds clear spiritual goals in the church program, parents would do well to consider the same for their own families.

listen to this. *Traits of great parents.*[3] What do young people say about good parenting? Here are some quotes that clarify.

() "Loving acceptance; concerned with all areas of the child's life; encouraging presence—encouraging not just with words, but also by their time and presence."

() "One who is involved in teens' lives. One who truly cares about whether their children succeed. Cares enough to tell a child he is wrong."

() "Genuine and honest, full of love and truth; insightful in understanding where their teen is at; dedicated and committed."

( ) "They set rules and make clear to the teen the purpose of those rules. They also need to share the struggles they had as teens. The parents need to be there for support if the teen fails or has questions."

( ) "Parents who are real with their teens and show them that they are trying their best to walk with Christ also. Good communicators!"

helping personal piety

So after the primary issues of helping parents be the kind of people that reflect Christ, and reminding church members to model the kingdom of God, how do you get young people actually involved in a deep, personal relationship with God? How do you build a close, personal friendship with the Savior that moves one to care and encourages compassionate service, upholding and joining in the community of saints?

In our research, personal piety—Bible study, prayer, engagement with others in community service, for example—is a crucial element in faith maturity and personal denominational loyalty. These close correlations make us recognize that a strong vertical relationship with God should flow into concern for others and assisting to build a community of compassionate, responsible people working together to share their vision of God's will in the world.

The Apostle Paul draws the same conclusion as he discusses his goal for ministry. It was to "proclaim him, admonishing and teaching everyone with all wisdom, so that we may present everyone perfect in Christ." (Colossians 2:28).

Let's look more closely at the goals for spiritual life in a church as they relate to young people and see what we can do to help young people get involved. We begin with our identified goal number one.

1. Assist in developing a close, personal friendship with Jesus. This is best understood by looking at how Jesus taught his disciples. During the years that Jesus was on earth he used contemporary methods to share his understanding of the Father in heaven. For example, Jesus would act and the disciples watched. As he healed, talked to people on the edge of society, interacted with the authorities of the time, and approached children as equals, His methods reflected an important learning theory that most educators understand and integrate into the best types of education today. Just talk to any competent elementary school teacher and you'll see how much this method is central to good teaching of any secular subject.

(a) *Theorists recognize that people learn best by relationships, interactions, involvement, and observation.* The Bible is filled with this type of learning experience.

Jesus was to be our example, walking with His values and modeling His relationships as exemplary. It was His life that was to provide models of the values and attributes we need to survive in this world as Christians, His life that would provide the ideals by which we might live.

The Apostle Paul, again, like Jesus referred to his own life as a model echoing followers to do what he did. The New Testament book, Philippians, recommends this practice. *"Join with others in following my example, brothers, and take note of those who live according to the pattern we gave you."* (Philippians 3:17) Or look again at Philippians 4:9 where Paul says, *"Whatever you have learned or received or heard from me, or seen in me—put it into practice. And the God of peace will be with you."*

Early on in my study of faith development and acceptance of sound religious educational theory, I discovered this concept as important. Reading C. Ellis Nelson's book *Where Faith Begins*, I learned that faith should be seen residing in the community of faith (the church) and is therefore exampled or modeled for new members. Nelson believed that Jesus presented "ideals" that the world could benefit by and that the church might use as a credo to model the kingdom.[4]

(b) *People who love God are the best teachers.* On the first day in my class in faith development at the university I begin by asking each young adult how they came to faith. When you ask them to identify the factors that had a strong influence on their spiritual growth, most often they name someone they know. Often it will be a pastor, local leader, parent, or grandparent. Seldom do I hear that some concept about God or even a powerful sermon had an influence. It is usually always a person. Their character and personality and life demonstrate the values youth want to incorporate into their lives.

It is because of this that the process of modeling is important. Perry Downs, in his book *Teaching for Spiritual Growth,* states that "A purely formal, cognitive approach to education can allow the teacher to teach in a detached way, not allowing the truth to penetrate his or her life. The possibility of 'academic objectivity' can cause truth to be taught in impersonal, sterile ways. But when the teacher must be a model of what is being taught, there must be a deeper involvement with the truth. Content can no longer be taught in abstract, detached ways."[5] This is why people are important. They are lived faith.

2. *Invite young people to follow Christ.* One of the best methods of assisting young people to develop a personal relationship is to invite them to accept Christ and follow him. The disciples responded to a personal invitation. We know that young people have a sense of spirituality; this new generation is interested in religion at the personal level. Postmodern young people want to get personally involved, so it is imperative that the local congregation take the time to invite them to get involved.

This is not an appeal for an emotional approach or altar call. Many times these emotional appeals do not initiate deep, personal involvement, and are more coercion than response. To avoid this, try to keep these types of calls to a minimum. Instead, take the time to get to know the young people and invite them to think seriously about their growth and relationship and its implications in the life. Friends always talk about important things, so it is crucial that the relationship exists before you remind them of God's purpose in their lives.

If following God seems relevant and useful, the invitation is often accepted or at least considered. Simply putting an announcement in the church bulletin is not enough. A personal contact, a personal invitation is what is needed.

In a course on personal faith I have been teaching for a number of years, I ask each student to write a journal. This personalization of what has been taught, allowing time for reflection and personal application of the concepts given, has been most fruitful as a means of invitation to find God. If young people are never asked to become friends of Jesus, they just may not ever make a personal decision. So look for opportunities during teaching sessions, sermons, lessons, sports events, mission trips to ask the personal question, "How do you feel about your relationship to Jesus?" Or "Have you make any decisions about Jesus lately?" And never forget that every Bible study or outing should have a moment of personal reflection so people can make some sort of relevant response.

3. *Involve young people that don't seem very involved.* Every

church has a list of young people that "used" to be active. This list often sits idle in the church office. And just like what is needed at the beginning of building a ministry, you have to find the youth in order to invite then to be involved.

try this. *Take a Census.* Take a look at the demographics of your local church.

() What percentage of young people of various ages are represented in the census of your church. Is it 10%? Is the statistic more like 25%?

() Then, evaluate the officers in the church, committee memberships, leaders, and teachers in all divisions, and ask this question: "What would it take to get these young people fully represented in this church?"

() Ask the church board to consider more youth involvement in local church activities and leadership.

The invitation to get involved in the life of the church may be all that is needed to get young people who were inactive more involved and open for the Holy Spirit to come into their lives to begin a personal relationship with Jesus.

"People will imitate those with whom they have a relationship. Education that is powerful stresses both content and relationships. . . . Paul could urge the church at Corinth to imitate him because he had a relationship with them. At the writing of the second epistle the relationship was not good, but even then he appealed to the example he had been in their midst."[6] Relationships are always the foundation for quality socialization and young people will not imitate people that they don't like!

If the church is to involve their young people in a personal relationship, it must learn to naturally imitate members that show love for God and others. If they don't see this kind of life in their church, where else will they seek to find it?

4. *Don't forget the head and the heart as you share Jesus.* Thinking and feeling are not separate approaches to God. Both are intimately connected. Reason informs faith and thinking logically should impact behavior, as does emotional commitment to a cause or purpose. Both are important. Involving young people means caring for both.

Young people, as they move to the personalizing stages of

faith development, need to clarify their ideology through careful study, growth in their own intellect, and careful understanding of the role and purpose of Scripture. While at the same time they are learning to grow intellectually, they are maturing emotionally and we want to learn how they feel as well as how they think. Leaving one out for the benefit of the other is irresponsible to the whole person.

As you plan to involve young people in a personal relationship with Jesus, balance both the intellectual approach with that of experiential ones. As young people get older, the rational slowly grows, but may never take over the whole person as an approach to change.

Approaching commitment using rational, logical propositional truth or doctrinal understanding provides a good foundation for decisions, but making sure that these same truths are relevant and touch the young person's heart, soul, and spirit is equally needed.

This is why worship becomes a crucial approach to the heart of the young. This is why praise music, which represents an outpouring of one's love to God, is so powerful to young people. Church hymns, on the other hand, often declare truth and support religious beliefs rather than move one to direct their attention to the author and finisher of our faith. Now, this is not a rationale for a theology of music, only an observation relative to the needs and understanding of the age of youth.

5. Teach growing young Christians who can filter life through a Christian worldview. It's all about choices. Whether you are at a party where alcohol and other drugs are available, being pressured to have sex, or joining a gang, or even simply being tempted to cheat on a math exam., making the right decisions is the practical side of being a Christian.

People of mature faith are learning how to make good choices based on clear biblical values. However, if a church or caring adults and parents support and guide them as they make important decisions, their future is more secure.

There seem to be two basic types of choices: one, those we make freely; and, two, those that are made for us. An example of both are the biblical stories surrounding the life of Moses, the castaway child found in the Nile River and raised up as a ruler of Egypt. Moses was not involved in the choice of his childhood. Those choices were made by his parents for all kinds of reasons. But as he grew and learned more, there was a transition in his life.

Now he was responsible for the decision he made and for his subsequent actions.

Wealth or poverty? God's way, or the way of the Pharaohs of Egypt? And it was at the burning bush, after some bad choices, that he and God reached an agreement of who was going to be in charge of his life. After some discussion and dissension about his future, he settled on God as Lord. From that decision on, a lot changed in Moses' life.

We could cite others—Joseph, Daniel, Peter, and Paul. All experienced changed lives, close relationships with God, and new ways to live because of their choice to follow God.

People of faith learn to make the right choices. How much better to learn that in the context of a church family who cares rather than in the world, or with people that have other priorities?

How can a church and the home help in this process when it is somewhat normal for young people to challenge their parents' values, beliefs, and practices as a way to test parents and assert their independence? After all, young people need support and guidance from their parents to make important decisions about their future. We know, for example, that the more controlling parents are, the more rebellious teens are often likely to become. So what can we do?

tips for the church and parents. Check these out and see if you can use any of these suggestions to help young people form a Christian worldview.

() Allow your young people to talk about the problem or situation. Keep open the channels of communication.

() Talk about making choices. This is a responsibility of caring adults and parents.

() Help your youth identify and compare the possible consequences of all the choices.

() Help your young to make a decision and support them as they attempt to carry it out.

() Later, ask how things worked out. Follow up with some sort of responsible feedback.

() Help young people build self-esteem and self-respect; it helps them make more responsible, healthy, choices.

() Talk to your young people about ways to handle risky situations and prepare him or her to make safe choices.

() Never punish them for being honest. Be a part of creating a warm, accepting place where youth feel comfortable talking and testing their choices.

Remember, living a life of faith is full of choices; it creates a Christian worldview. God gives us all the chance to make good choices and bad ones. God gives us this freedom, but at the same time He challenges us that if we want a full life, one with unbelievable opportunities, we should choose God.

We too often feel we are stuck in our past, a product of our time. And because of our sins, we don't think there is much hope for us, or that we might never be able to live a truly victorious Christian life. Don't feel alone. Almost 70 percent of youth surveyed feel the same way.

Some young people say, "Christianity may work for others, but is doesn't work for me." But according to Colossians 3:9-11, how we identified ourselves before we accepted Christ no longer applies. *"Do not lie to each other, since you have taken off your old self with its practices and have put on the new self, which is being renewed in knowledge in the image of its Creator. Here there is no Greek or Jew, circumcised or uncircumcised, barbarian, Scythian, slave or free, but Christ is all, and is in all."*

Your teen's physical heritage, social standing, racial distinctions, or sins no longer determine their identity. Their identity lies in the fact that they are a child of God and are in Christ. When they decide to put trust in Christ, they gain forgiveness from every sin they would ever commit because Christ died once for all of their sins. And the church and its people, parents and grandparents, brothers and sisters must reinforce this wonderful truth and help them see the value of Christ's sacrifice for their future.

6. Deepening knowledge of God's word and understanding of its truths.

Another goal to meet if involvement in the church is to be attained is that of helping young people see the power and help provided by understanding God's Word and clarifying its truths, making them relevant to their own lives. This is a challenge to the church itself as well as to Christian education.

Bible study and doctrinal instruction is a central part of any organized religion. Teaching for theological development is one goal, but another is on the practical side: to understand the Bible so as to inform one's life is more central to the goal we have of involving youth in the church.

If young people are able to attend a denominational school

where the Bible is a daily part of the curriculum, they may very well have an advantage. Here they will see models of how people sort out actions from Bible stories and make personal applications. If, on the other hand, your young people come primarily from public education, your challenge is greater. The weekly meetings of the youth group may very well be the only exposure they have on a regular basis to learn the art of biblical exposition and application to their lives. So churches must take this task seriously.

Instruction must be on their own age-level so they can understand it. "For example, teaching the concept of the Trinity to most early adolescents and to many middle adolescents is often a waste of time. They are not cognitively capable of understanding such an abstract concept. In fact, many adults have a difficult time comprehending the Trinity. Instruction, to be effective, must be understandable developmentally before it can be acted upon."[7]

In the local church and home there are many opportunities to use the concept of instruction as a model of learning about God. Do a survey of these opportunities; you will probably find a number of them, such activities as weekly Bible school programs, worship preaching services, Bible study nights, devotional times, evangelistic meetings, youth groups, summer camps, weekend retreats, counseling, and one-on-one-discipleship contacts are such opportunities.

For some churches, however, this is all they do. Instruction and assent to truth discussions are the total focus of their ministry, forgetting the other aspects of young people's concern. Often every meeting contains some directive teaching activity. But remember, content alone does not save anyone and memorized key texting of doctrines and hours of Bible study do not in any way guarantee a deeply devotional and spiritual life.

What does an instructional approach do? There are positive aspects to this task too. This approach helps people see clearly what God's values and will for their lives might be. It also clarifies some of the deep religious questions—the nature of Christ, the day of worship, the ministry of Christ, the state of the dead are examples of this.

try this. *Bible Beliefs Survey.*[8] Give this quick survey to your young people about what they believe. They can select answers from "I have never heard of this" to "I definitely believe this." See how well your youth do with these doctrinal questions. (Feel free to modify these questions to reflect your denominational viewpoint.) A copy of this survey is available in the "Extra" sections at the end of this book.

1. God created the world in six 24-hour days
   - ○ I definitely disagree
   - ○ I tend to disagree
   - ○ I'm not sure
   - ○ I tend to agree
   - ○ I definitely agree

2. Jesus will come back to earth again and take the righteous to heaven
   - ○ I definitely disagree
   - ○ I tend to disagree
   - ○ I'm not sure
   - ○ I tend to agree
   - ○ I definitely agree

3. The Ten Commandments still apply to us today
   - ○ I definitely disagree
   - ○ I tend to disagree
   - ○ I'm not sure
   - ○ I tend to agree
   - ○ I definitely agree

4. The true Sabbath is the seventh day—Saturday
   - ○ I definitely disagree
   - ○ I tend to disagree
   - ○ I'm not sure
   - ○ I tend to agree
   - ○ I definitely agree

5. When people die, they remain in the grave until the resurrection
   - ○ I definitely disagree
   - ○ I tend to disagree
   - ○ I'm not sure
   - ○ I tend to agree
   - ○ I definitely agree

5. The wicked will not burn forever, but will be totally destroyed
   - ○ I definitely disagree
   - ○ I tend to disagree
   - ○ I'm not sure
   - ○ I tend to agree
   - ○ I definitely agree

6. The body is a temple of God and we are responsible for its care
   - ○ I definitely disagree

- I tend to disagree
- I'm not sure
- I tend to agree
- I definitely agree

7. I know that to be saved I have to live by God's rules
   - I definitely disagree
   - I tend to disagree
   - I'm not sure
   - I tend to agree
   - I definitely agree

8. The way to be accepted by God is to try sincerely to live a good life
   - I definitely disagree
   - I tend to disagree
   - I'm not sure
   - I tend to agree
   - I definitely agree

9. I am loved by God even when I sin
   - I definitely disagree
   - I tend to disagree
   - I'm not sure
   - I tend to agree
   - I definitely agree

10. I am worried abut not being ready for Christ's return
    - I definitely disagree
    - I tend to disagree
    - I'm not sure
    - I tend to agree
    - I definitely agree

Time spent in worship and loving fellowship along with active community involvement through service become important teaching tools to clarify what believing certain things means in real life.

But instruction is only one of the steps in a balanced ministry to the young in the church. Remember, heart and head are important. So spend some time thinking about how much time you spend in only instructional tasks. If you want involvement, do a good job here, make the instruction relevant to their own lives, and build on these discussions to ask the question of how knowing these truths plays out in making real decisions as youth live every day trying to be the believing Christians the church has so carefully explored. This discussion logically leads us to the next goal for church young people.

7. Encourage the application of biblical insights into daily living. This goal is another natural transition from the one above. Study of the Bible is *only* helpful if application takes place. There are three steps in discovering an application of a biblical text in this process.

Step 1. What was the original meaning of the text?

Step 2. What is the universal principle?

Step 3. What does it mean to me?

Each of these steps informs the next one. And while we may think that our life is very different from the way life was lived in Bible times, many things remain the same. People had to make a living, build families, discover eternal values, learn to put God first in their lives, explore feelings about religion, fight against excesses in personal life, get along with others, develop faith, learn to find their personal mission in life, explore their own personalities, develop a devotional life.[9]

And as we look at the biblical stories, we recognize that we still need to learn how to love God before others. Husbands and wives still need to learn to care for each other and put their families first. The feelings of loneliness and being lost still creep into our lives, just as they did to Elijah when he was fleeing Jezebel. Nevertheless, we cannot ignore the fact that the Bible was written long ago and for a different historical time. This is what makes the biblical application process especially challenging. "Getting into the skin of the Bible writers is the key."[10]

Teach the youth of your church to see how relevant the Bible still is by using these three steps. Young people will become involved in study of the Bible if, and that is a big "if," we learn that relevancy is the key. Does it say anything to me? How can I use this for my life today? Does it answer my contemporary questions? So what? All these concerns melt away if we try to find out what the text says in its deepest sense.

Now, there are other ways to do this. In Chap Clark and Kara Powell's book, *Deep Ministry in a Shallow World,* they posit a four-step process to dig deeper into the will of God.

"Step 1 "(Discernment): Now?—Try to sense God's will.

Step 2 (Reflection): New?—What is new to you today?

Step 3 (Observation): Who?—How do you see God at work?

Step 4 (Application): How?"—Making it work in your life.[11]

However you do it, let me suggest that you begin. Involvement in the church happens when what happens there is relevant and important to people's lives. Youth, who are just developing opinions and beliefs and making choices that impact their future, need to be in a place where relevant and practical Scripture study happens. Then, and only then will the application of these biblical insights move into their daily life choices.

try this. *Bible Application to Real Life.* Here are some Bible stories that you can share with young people. Have everyone read the story in their Bibles, then ask someone to tell it in their own words. Break into small groups of no more than three people and answer this question, "What does this story have to say to my life today?"

( ) The story of Jonah's hilltop view (Jonah 3-4)
( ) The story of a child's hearing God (1 Samuel 3: 1-20)
( ) The building of a wall (Nehemiah 4)
( ) A storm story (Luke 8:22-25)
( ) A hungry crowd (John 6)
( ) A brand new city (Revelation 21)

8. Involvement in sharing Christ through life, work, service and witness.

Every action requires a reaction. This is a truism in science, but it is just as true regarding religion. Once a commitment is made there are results. In John 3 the famous story of Nicodemus' night visit to Jesus exhibits this same fact. In the middle of Jesus' concerns about the nature of the new birth he illustrates this fact by saying that the Holy Spirit can be seen by the results that are manifest. Commitment to God produces something. One's life, vocation, involvement with others, and one's desire to share what one knows about God moves logically from the commitments one makes.

Our chapter, "Getting Involved in Compassionate Care," takes this goal of church life for youth seriously, so we won't say more here except that the truth of God's power to change is seen in the results in the life.

One way to test the power of God is to see if things are different now, in contrast to what was before one's commitment became focused on Christ. Just what is the movement in the life? What new concerns seem to be moving to the center of one's concerns? How have things changed? And, remember, not all of the changes may be positive. Often when we make commitments that stretch us, we find that others don't appreciate it the same way we do.

Another aspect of this element centers on the church's responsibility to teach its members how to witness and share their testimony. If you want young people involved, they need some direction in this area. In our earlier discussion we introduced the concept of faith-talk. Remember, this is when you talk about what God is doing for you. Often we think that sharing or witnessing is trying to get someone else to believe the way we do, or to join a church like ours. However, faith-talk is personal, direct, and authoritative because it shares only what you know to be true in your life.

try this. *Faith-talk Testimony.* It is not hard to teach young people as well as church members how to share their witness with others. Use this rubric and see if your sharing becomes more personal and direct.

1. Ask yourself, "What is God doing in my life?" Write it down.

2. Ask yourself, "How have I seen God work over the past year in my life?" Write it down.

3. Get in groups of two and share your answers.

4. Try to talk to your partner about God's work over the years in your life. How you have felt, and what has happened to you or your family or friends who have known God.

Now you have a testimony that can be shared as a witness to God's power and life.

This element of response to God's call can take many turns and has many aspects. For example, service can be the focal point, "the place where learning can be formed on a cognitive-affective-social-spiritual-behavioral base."[12] Choosing a direction in your life (work) can become an answer to God's calling; while at the same time, one's witness can reflect the excitement of new commitments and give new motivation to sharing with your friends and family.

9. Instill a faith that can function in daily life apart from the church and family. This concept is an expression of transference. We don't mean what is usually thought of as transference according to Sigmund Freud and psychoanalytic theory, but simply what takes place when we use something we learned earlier in life at some later appropriate time.

We may *know* some facts or beliefs, or perform some behaviors, but we may not have *learned* them. Only knowing something is not the same as true learning.

We have a joke in our family. We often, after hearing a sermon or lecture, say to each other, "He knows lots of stuff about stuff." Transference is the concept that describes remembering what you have learned and incorporating the concept or activity into your daily life. You might say it this way: "A habit is a transferred knowing."

We learn through repetition of the activity, or reflection on the concept and previous experience and knowledge. That is why in the Christian life, we say it is important to have a faith that can function when we are away from the church and the home. When you are alone, only with yourself and your thoughts, what do you think and how do you behave? When you are with your friends and business associates, do you act the same, believe the same, and talk the same? It's the "Walk the walk," and "Talk the talk," type of concern. There should be some consistency between what the church teaches and how each of us lives apart from the church and away from our families.

getting them involved

Helping your young people learn how to develop a personal relationship with God is one of the priorities any family, church, or youth or young adult ministry should target.

Putting young people's spiritual life at the center of your church's concerns is the way to begin. Here is a summary of what we have been talking about. See how many of these elements are already in your youth and family ministry.

First, how well does your church focus on building a strong parents network and ministry? As parents, youth leaders, or pastors, have you helped in growing spiritual kids by targeting personal piety?

Second, has your church made any commitment to:

() Assist youth develop a close, personal friendship with Jesus;

() Teach young Christians to filter life through a Christian worldview;

() Assist young people with their knowledge of God's word and understanding of its truths;

() Encouraged the application of biblical insights into daily living;

() Involved young people in sharing Christ through life, work, service and witness;

() Helped to instill a faith that can function in daily life apart from the church and family in their heart.

While these goals are lofty, they are crucial if we are ever going to build a community of compassionate and loving people that feel the responsibility to assist in the nurture of the young in their care. But however your church decides to get involved will be a benefit to the whole community. The young will see role models in the church working for others and catch a vision of what a Christian should do. The youth in the church will get a taste of what active love is all about and they will begin to talk about their experiences, feelings, and accomplishments which will only bring a new sense of identity and Christian worldview. The young adults who actively participate in compassionate caring discover just how they might act when they are in charge of their church in the future. The adults learn the importance of modeling the Kingdom of God. Everyone wins and the Kingdom of God just might grow.

chapter 5 / endnotes

1. Ken Curtis, (2006) "How the Journey turned my life and ministry upside down," *Adventist Today On-Line* accessed on 11/13/06 at: <http://www.atoday.com/56.0.html>.

2. Adapted in part from Joe White, Jim Weidmann, eds. *Parents' Guide to the Spiritual Mentoring of Teens* (Wheaton, IL: Tyndale House Publishers, 2001), 656-66.

3. Joe White, Jim Weidmann, eds. *Parents' Guide*, 61.

4. See C. Ellis Nelson, *Where Faith Begins* (Louisville, KY: John Knox Press, 1967.

5. Perry G. Downs, *Teaching for Spiritual Growth: An Introduction to Christian Education* (Grand Rapids, MI: Zondervans, 1994), 161.

6. Perry G. Downs, *Spiritual Growth*, 166.

7. John M. Dettoni, *Introduction to Youth Ministry,* (Grand Rapids, MI: Zondervans, 1993), 29.

8. This survey was adapted from scales in the *Valuegenesis[2] (Revised College/ University Short Form: A study of the influence of the family, college/ university and church on the formation of faith among young adults.* (Riverside, CA: Hancock Center for Youth and Family Ministry, 2005). 3-4. These questions were originally a part of the *Valuegenesis[1]* research project by the North American Division of Seventh-day Adventists. National norms can be found in, V. Bailey Gillespie, Michael J. Donahue with Ed Boyatt and

Barry Gane, *Ten Years Later: A Study of Two Generations* (Lincoln, NE: AdventSource, 2004) available from: www.hancockcenterstore.com.

9. V. Bailey Gillespie, *To Make Us Wise: How to Make Bible Study Relevant to Yout Life Today* (Boise, ID: Pacific Press, 1995), 77-78.

10. V. Bailey Gillespie, *To Make Us Wise*, 79.

11. Chap Clark, Kara E. Powell, *Deep Ministry in a Shallow World* (Grand Rapids, MI: Zondervans, 2006), 25.

12. John M. Dettoni, *Introduction to Youth Ministry*, 105.

chapter 6

getting involved in worship

The Sacred Hour—11 am-12 pm. No place for Kids, right? Wrong! Could there be a better place to lift up the young people of the church? Could there be a better time as a community when we can acknowledge, encourage, and train young people in our faith story and mold their excitement—shape their commitments? If we are truly searching for ways to involve young people in church life, then it is impossible to ignore the weekly focus of worship as a place where the young can become involved.

You have probably heard all of the arguments against young people's involvement in the worship service. Let's review some of them.

() They don't *look* like they should be up in front of church.
() They don't *prepare* in a way that is appropriate for their participation.
() We don't really have *anything* for them to do.
() They are hard to *depend* on.
() They don't *listen* to the same music we do; sometimes it feels like they don't even speak the same language we do.
() They wouldn't be interested in *helping* us out with our worship service.
() We have created a *special service* for them so they don't have to sit through our services.

These are just a few of the reasons that are given when we speak of young people being involved. They have felt their isolation and are well aware that church is often not for kids. The truth is, often we are so bound to traditional worship styles and programming we have simply forgotten to involve our young people in our services at any level. While this is no one's fault, we have to work to change that church paradigm that has neglected to include the young in worship. The great thing is, it is much easier than you think to get them involved in worship at your church.

The first thing we have to remember is that they are in church too. And the real question becomes, what are we doing to program for these various ages in our weekly worship service? Week after week we ask the young to sit through a church service, which has very little relevance to them. It is almost as if they become second-class citizens who just have to sit and wait for something that might appeal to them.

Of course, the argument goes something like this: "church is not entertainment; they should endure it even if they don't like it." But let's ask the real personal question. "Would you?" Is it fair to ask young people to try and be engaged in something that they hardly understand? Would you continue to be interested in something that didn't speak to you after months or years? I don't believe it is fair to ask someone to continue to suffer through programming that is not targeted at their needs or interests when we have the power to make a few changes that would plug them into the service in a new and vital way.

Let's look at two different aspects of the worship service where we can easily involve young people so that they feel as if they have become a central part of that service. The first is *participation in the service itself*, and the second is *involvement behind the scenes.*

what to do up front

While there is always a risk involved in putting anyone new on the rostrum or platform of the local church, with the right kind of coaching, however, even the most shy or inexperienced person can begin to excel and start to succeed in their own way. Let's look at the many elements of worship where young people can be easily become integrated into church worship.

Music. There is a good chance you have a great deal of talent among your young people in your church; it just needs to be brought out. Many know who in their church has musical talent; however, there are many who have not had a chance to share their gift with others. There are lots of reasons for this, but often it is simply because no one has asked them to share, or the talent is hidden under a bushel, as the song goes. The Bible shares that God gives gifts to his children, so why not try to get these out in the open by identifying them, using a gift registration for the whole church.

try this. *Gifts registration.* How do you begin? A great way to start this search is to hand out an information card. It could look like this:

Talent Questionnaire. Give us some important information about your interests and gifts.

( ) Do you play an instrument?

( ) What instrument?

( ) How long have you been playing?

( ) Can you read music, or simply work from chord charts?

( ) Who is your music teacher?

( ) Would you be interested in helping out with music for worship at our church?

Once you have figured out which young people are interested in music and what instruments they play, all you need to do is plug them in.

When you do your research among the young people and young adults in your church, anything from special music to playing along with the organ is possible. Regardless of the worship style your church employs, there are opportunities for young people to get involved in worship music. It is probable that you already have a young person or two who get involved in special music, and that is great. However, don't discount those who, while not interested in solos, would be interested in working with a group to lead a hymn or a praise and worship set. Church families love the concept of seeing their young people in leadership roles, and will sometimes be more amenable to a new song or a song that is not typically what your church would use for worship. Never underestimate the power of grandchildren on opening the eyes of their grandparents either. If young people are involved up front in making and presenting music, everyone grows and begins to appreciate each other.

For a list of songs currently being used by many youth groups and contemporary churches currently, go to www.worshiptogether.com

and look at their top ten list of songs. This is a perfect way for young people to introduce a new song to the congregation, as well as allowing them to feel ownership and relevancy to their personal worship experience. But finding out your church's gifts is just the beginning of involvement.

try this. *Kids' Choir.* Create a children's choir for a song that will work specifically with the theme of the sermon. The song should be short and include some hand motions, especially if the mean age of the choir is very young. This allows parents to get involved in ministry with the children. It is a good way to get your church comfortable with young people on the platform. And, believe me, all parents love to see their children up front in church, even if the presentation is simple and easy.

Scripture lessons. Don't forget the scripture lesson. You can be creative here and involve lots of young people and their parents as role models. This is perhaps the easiest way for young people to become involved in the platform service is to allow them to read or enact scripture. While this is a relative low-stress assignment, it still needs coaching to help the young person become comfortable in their presentation. I always find that it is important to have the young person practice from the pulpit in an empty church with the public address system on. This gives them a sense of what it will be like on Sabbath morning.

You can also become more and more creative with the scripture reading from week to week. Responsive readings where there is a section for those who are under the age of 15 or 18, having a voice choir for different texts that are highlighted. (See our resource section on voice choirs and creative scripture readings called "extras"). If the text is short, it is always fun to see the younger Sabbath School classes come up and be a part of the program.

Act it out with drama. And what about drama in your church? Some churches are a bit nervous about this type of creative exercise, but done right it can be an inspirational part of any worship service. There are a number of resources in this area as well. And if your church has never done drama before, using the scripture as a starting point is an easy and important way to begin involving young people.

"When people act out a biblical story, they notice aspects of the narrative that they might miss otherwise," Sandra Costen Kunz says. "Perhaps this is the reason Ignatius Loyola recommended a type of meditation on Scripture where one sets the stage for the narrative in one's imagination—envisioning each character, action, emotion, *et cetera.*"[1]

Done correctly, drama, reader's theater, and scripture readings can be a powerful way to integrate the young in worship. After all, God the creator, who made all things good, did it with color and variety and vision. He made us a people who learn better through audio and visual means. And Jesus built on this trait as he shared the parables and even in the Last Supper where he gave a visual representation of just what God was saying to everyone who was there. You can't go far away from the prophets of the Old Testament, Jeremiah, Ezekiel, and Isaiah and not see the drama and visualization of the power of God's words. And as we help the young express themselves, what better content is there than the Bible.

The Bible is the best source. Use the New Testament and the Parables of Jesus, share the feelings of the different people Jesus met in his sojourn, relive the situations that the Apostle Paul was in, and try sharing the images of the end times seen in the Book of Revelation. The Old Testament is a rich resource too. The Psalms are full of creative ideas, or using Genesis you could mime the creation week or the issues facing Adam and Eve when they were banished from the Garden of Eden. Let your imagination run wild and get your young involved in sharing their gifts in scripture presentations rather than simply sharing a text.

But if you do only that, remember that you must use a translation of the text that is up-to-date and relevant to the people that are listening. There are many translations of the Biblical text that can be shared. Just remember, children don't have the same vocabulary as adults and your choice of scripture lessons must reflect that fact.

Prayer. A great idea to get a few different youth of various ages involved in the prayer from the front is to have three or four pray consecutively. This brings a new focus prayer in church, as well as hits different developmental levels. It shows the church that involvement is for everyone. It is important to coach these kids as well, and while they may not want to memorize their portion, it is good to have a general outline of what they will say. It is always nice to see the pastor in front with the students to perhaps bring it all together at the end. Don't forget the power of clear, directed worship leaders whether or not they are the pastor, head elder, or local member with gifts to lead others in prayer.

try this. *Bidding prayers.* You have to practice this, however, because it is actually a very ancient style of public prayer. Have a child or youth read out loud some themes for silent prayer in the congregation. The young person says, "Let's give praise for love and life." (The congregation silently prays about this). Then the next bidding suggestion comes, "Let's ask forgiveness for the things that separate us from God this week." (Again the congregation silently prays about this topic). And so it goes until the last benediction. A reverse of the "Bidding Prayer" model would be when the pastor or prayer elder gives the cue, but individual children, youth, and parents answer the bidding suggestion.

Call to Offering. This time in the service has a tendency to be relatively businesslike and less creative. Getting young people involved in this aspect of the service can be rewarding both monetarily and in nurturing relationships. There are a myriad of ways to present this topic to the church family, and having kids involved usually soothes this often given repeated message of stewardship. One the first things that needs to be done is to educate those who will be involved on where the money goes when it comes through the offering plates. It is both informative to the kids and allows them to feel more connected to the world church. Here are some creative ways to involve your young people in this aspect of worship.

try this. *Duct Tape Plate.* Get some duct tape and have your young people make two or more (depending on the size and layout of your church). Strips that are the length of a pew in your church. Then, instead of passing the offering plate, instruct your members to stick their money or tithe envelopes, even checks, to the tape as it comes over their heads while the youth move slowly back to the rear of your sanctuary. It is important to have your young people practice this before you bring it into the service; no one wants their hair stuck in duct tape. We guarantee your giving will go up the week you try this.

try this. *The gift-wrap.* Call for offering something like this. Ask all the members of the church to get a coin out of their purse or pocket and put it in their hands. Make sure everyone in the congregation has a coin, and then talk about gift-giving and ask them to gift-wrap the coin with a piece of paper money. If they want to be really creative, they can even use colored paper (checks)!

try this. *The pie chart.* You will need a big piece of poster board for this call for offering: Have a young person, wearing a suit, bring up a large pie chart and begin to explain how the different parts of a dollar are divided throughout the church. Then, to make it more relevant, have him or her bring out an actual pie, and cut it up into pieces. Then give the pieces away after church.

try this. *The allowance.* Bring up a young person to interview about his or her allowance: As you discuss where the money ends up that is given in tithe, have them help you with the math of their allowance. The congregation will appreciate the math prowess of the young person, and it is a very practical illustration.

Welcome and Announcements. Too often this part of the program falls into a rut. And these announcements, necessary and useful, clutter the worship experience or break up the worship flow. If you can't have them rolling up during the break between Sabbath School and church on an LCD projector, then the next best is to use that time to get more people involved with worship itself. With young people involved there is always something to look forward to. They can highlight the important information in a fresh and new way, as well as welcome the church and invite them to worship. As always, it is important make sure they are prepared. Our job as enablers includes the preparation so that a student is enabled to succeed, and to feel comfortable when on the platform.

try this! *Sharing Announcements.* Have a different young person give each different announcement. This allows for more kids on the platform and it also creates a sense of camaraderie among the young people on the platform. It is even possible to create a skit that they might want to do in order to peak the interest of the congregation. For instance, have two 8-year olds invite each other to the potluck after church; then have them invite the entire congregation.

Preaching. This is perhaps the toughest portion of the service to give away to anyone else. If you are like most pastors or worship leaders, this is the time when your membership gets a vision of life and spiritual presence in your congregation. While this is a very important time for the pastor and the congregation, it is also a wonderful time to allow your congregation to hear from your young people. However, as in all we do with young people, there is a great deal of work that needs to go into preparing a student for this opportunity. Assume you need to take just as much time as you would preparing for any sermon when you work with a young person preparing their talks.

When you are young, you don't realize just how long 25-30 minutes is. It is an incredibly long time for most young people to speak at any time, much less to the people in church. In fact, they can easily see this as overwhelming. Therefore, it is always nice to break up the speaking portion of the service among two to four young people. It is also important to make sure they understand the theme for the week, and what the other young people will be saying so there is not redundancy. Take all these young people out to lunch early in the week and talk about what you would like to see them speak about. At the end of the lunch they should be clear on what they need to prepare. As well, schedule a meeting for Thursday or Friday in which they will go over their talk with you. It is great if they can practice on Friday or Friday night in the pulpit so they can become more comfortable as they get closer to their speaking engagement. Listen to their talks and remember, they do not have the training you do, so be kind and not overly critical. They will appreciate the support, but it really should be their talk, not one you have dictated to them.

Remember, our *Valuegenesis* research indicates that one real challenge for the church of today is letting the youth see how important they are through creative involvement, warm climates, and an appreciation of critical thinking skills. Helping them develop the ability to be used by the Spirit of God in presenting the message to the membership shares these concerns in a real way.

behind the scenes

There are so many elements that must come together in order for a worship service to work smoothly. Your young people can become an invaluable resource in making sure the service comes off without a hitch. Also, it can occupy them and give them more of a reason to be in the sanctuary when the service begins. Too many times we have had our young people in the hallways or parking lot rather than in the pews. While this may not put them in the pews, it will certainly give them ownership of the service.

High and low tech. Simply put, your young people are very proficient in today's technology; they have to be to survive. With this in mind, why not create some opportunities for them at church to use their technical prowess. With very little investment, your church can have computer-generated projections to help with the flow of service. From the words to hymns and praise music, to the projection of announcements, these young people can man the computer, set up the projector, create the presentation, and keep a database of the files needed.

If budget is an issue (as it is in every church I've ever been to) enlist the help of church members who might be getting rid of an old computer, one that can handle either Power Point presentations or Media Shout (which this author highly recommends). The purchase of a video card is a relatively cheap investment, while the purchase of a projector can be expensive. If you have a school somehow affiliated with your church, there may be a possibility of them having a projector you could purchase or borrow. However, you will not be disappointed for a few different reasons:

Your young people can get involved in a ministry that requires some responsibility.

() It brings up the level of programming in your church service.

() It helps the church think in a forward direction when it comes to technology.

() Along with this new technology comes a new interested in the digital video medium. Many young people today own or have access to a digital still camera or a digital video camera. They can be enlisted to take pictures of church services, activities, potlucks, or even video the church service to become a resource for those who are unable to be in church on a weekly basis. It can quickly become a wonderful form of outreach for your young people. Since your youth or young adults have access to computers, it will be a snap for them to become proficient in editing the service down to its main elements. As they get excited about the opportunity, you will see an influx of support for this ministry. My bet is that they will blow you away by how much they are willing and able to accomplish.

Since building a warm and accepting climate in church is one of the most important things you can do to grow a mature, rich and vibrant faith, the next component of this high/low tech ministry is something that almost every church struggles with.

Quality sound is crucial. That is, getting a quality sound system, and someone to run it. We won't go into what sort of system your church needs. That is something for which you need to seek professional advice. But young people can be a major resource when it comes to helping this ministry run smoothly. By training young people (I would recommend high school students, 15-18 years old) here you have a resource that will be around for a few years. You probably have a person in your congregation who can do the training, but if not, there is certainly someone in the community who, while you might have to pay, will certainly have the expertise to train.

Once the students are trained, get a schedule together of who will be on for each week, and then make sure you get them the sound needs (how many mics, special music with tracks, instruments needing to be plugged in, etc.) early in the week so the kids can be prepared come Sabbath morning. If you take them seriously in this responsibility, they will take their job seriously. It will be exciting to watch the young people take ownership of this ministry and strive toward excellence. Make sure you continually give them encouragement when things go well, and careful direction when they don't.

Pew management. Every church has a place where people sit. Whether it is pews or it is chairs, there are usually items that need to be placed into the pews. Things such as tithing envelopes, visitor cards, little pencils, bulletins and the like are simple to place, but time consuming. Go to your earliteen preteen or weekend youth study group and ask for a few volunteers who would like to make this ministry their own. The work is not hard, but you need someone to do it. It can be done before your group meeting or even between the study period and worship service as the youth learn to greet the older people in the congregation as they pass out these items and update the materials in the pews. The different groups might even be interested in making it a game and placing things in the pews each week such as gifts for visitors or cards of encouragement. Make sure you get a schedule together and a point person for each one of the groups. This can become a very creative and positive ministry for your church.

Never too young to help. Using young people to take up offering, welcome people, help with parking management, help older saints from their cars, and help with communion is always a positive experience both for the church and for the young people. These young people are voted into the office and are, or should be, assigned a mentor to learn from. Encourage the mentors to cultivate a relationship with these young people outside of the church setting. A lunch here or a dinner there can mean so much to a developing Christian. You have so many deep wells of wisdom in your church from which to pull, it would be a shame if they didn't get a chance to pass some of that wisdom on to the younger generations of the church. It may take some convincing of your deacons to step out on a limb and create a relationship with a teenager they may not have had a previous relationship with, but the results will be incredible for both mentor and young person.

try this. *Involvement Survey.* Here is a survey to use as a starting point to find out teen interest in church and what sort of commitment they might give you as a volunteer. .

1. How many times a month do you come to church?
2. Do your parents bring you, or do you drive yourself?
3. What are your hobbies at home?
4. Would you be interested in helping with a ministry here at the church?
5. Where do you think you could be the most help? (List your ministries below)
6. How can we get in touch with you?

Making some changes. We have on purpose not talked about building a creative youth-oriented worship services. We'll talk about this in a more biblical way later in this book, but for now remember that building a youth and young person friendly church is an intentional activity. It does not happen by chance or by default. Those churches where friendliness ruled the day were churches where their young people developed more loyalty and maturity than in churches where there were little activities or involvement in worship and where relevance in worship was not taken seriously.[2] So changing your church is a slow, necessary process, especially if you feel the young people have been neglected or even ignored in your church.

This may take some time for some churches to begin to change. One way to see if your church is ready for any drastic changes in worship is to gently approach this matter in the church board and then just see how long the discussion lasts! Often making subtle changes in the order of service, type of music, balance of age needs, and creative aspects of worship using both audio, visual, and stylistic changes causes tensions and stress for some in the church. But beginning somewhere is the best counsel we can provide. Start doing something that recognizes the importance of what can be the most valuable asset to the local congregation—the young people of your church—and get in touch with the hundreds of worship helps for young people on the World Wide Web.

chapter 6 / endnotes

1. Sandra Costen Kunz, Summer/Fall 2001. Volume 6 Number 1.2001 Princeton Theological Seminary. Assessed on-line at: <http://wwwptsem.edu/read/inspire/6.1/studentlife/SL2.html> or go to www.lillenasdrama.com for specific reader's theater on the Scriptures or books based on texts of the Old and New Testaments.

2. See V. Bailey Gillespie and Michael J. Donahue with Ed Boyatt and Barry Gane, *Ten Years Later: A Study of Two Generations* (Lincoln, NE: AdventSource, 2004).

3. Additional resources for teens and worship can be found at: <http://www.crosssearch.com/People/Youth/>; Worship resources for church life at: <http://www.lcms.org/pages/internal.asp?NavID=857>; The Calvin Institutie for Worship and Teens at: <http://www.calvin.edu/worship/worshipers/youth/>.

chapter 7

getting involved
in bible study

an important factor in building mature faith is learning to study the Bible as *the* important guide for life. One regular activity in which most congregations and families participate is learning the centrality of God's word for family, church, and personal decision-making and getting general guidelines about God's will, which suggest lifestyle choices. Bible study, along with church attendance patterns, are some of the key factors in identifying people as religious. There is a natural interface between young people and the church's responsibility to explore Scripture and its ability to teach others to apply biblical counsel to real-life situations.

When it comes to the youth in the church, there are some important basic skills needed if mastery in understanding the biblical text is the goal. In addition, to get them involved in the church, families as well as the church family need to model creative ways to look at scripture in order to meet personal motivational needs. Particularly in church, what is needed is to make sure that the adult leaders and volunteers have a basic understanding about the learning process so their time with young people will not be wasted. Teaching creative Bible study is a challenge for the whole church—leaders, parents, and each individual young person.

Professional educators involved in the instruction of teenagers are well aware of the basic motivators that operate in the interaction between learning and action (response). Here are six important concepts that motivate which need to be remembered and implemented

1. *Personal gain* — This primary motivator could be called personal benefit. People won't work for you or do things for you just because you ask. "Do this for me" is not particularly powerful in motivating others to action. If we add the extra motivation of need, "I need you to help me," this too may fail, but at some point most people, and especially teens, would like to know, "What's in it for me?" If you can show why something is important there is more involvement and interest. Don't forget this personal motivational need when you select sections of the biblical record to explore with your youth.

2. *Fear Avoidance* — The environment for getting involved must feel secure. There can be no embarrassment or feelings of isolation at church meetings or group gatherings. Young people are not going to want to learn if the environment is destructive to the learning experience. Often teens don't know their Bible at all. And it is easy to embarrass them or make them feel uneasy when we ask for biblical responses, or even for review of simple Bible stories. Remember, people avoid those things that make them feel insecure, so don't let your knowledge of the Bible intimidate those that don't know it well. Since a large portion of any teen congregation does not go to private Christian schools, the church must become the primary place where biblical learning skills are taught and used.

3. *Prestige* — Since learning is a personal activity, "prestige helps students gain recognition, win approval, and feel important."[1] If young people don't get positive feedback for their work, they feel put down or made to feel insignificant, and the result will be less motivation to accomplish and learn. Don't forget to praise each and every response, no matter how off the mark their answer might be. Creating a place where youth can feel recognized is an important identity function.

4. *Pleasure* — "I like it," is not the purest motivator, but it is realistic. This is one of the strongest motivators around. Teens want to enjoy their activities and when you are in an educational mode during church activities, you don't want to have the students thinking "Oh, no, school again." Think of how painful it must be for young people to be completely bored in church and then think

just how long eternity must really be. In applying this motivator in your Bible study, try to be creative and renew your method at regular intervals.

5. *Convenience* — It has been said that the fast food industry has made billions fulfilling this need. Learning has to be made easy and convenient. Long and hard assignments or "busywork" do not stimulate students and we often make learning harder than it needs to be. Keep your Bible study short, and to the point. Those churches that are the most successful with teen Bible study, are those that target one or two issues, develop clear biblical insights into the issues, and respect personal interpretations in light of good Bible study principles.

6. *Security* — We all need to feel safe and students are no different. All too often they are afraid about their grades, or their behaviors, or being uncomfortable in new surroundings or with people they don't know. If kids are worried that they might be in danger, even if that danger is purely psychological, it will impact their motivation and behaviors.

Thinking about what motivates people will have impact on how you teach and what you require. And teaching about the Bible can quickly move to simply a history lesson rather than motivating young people to see the Bible as the means whereby God talks to them today.

To add to the complexity of the possible motivators, recognize that each young person is an individual and various motivators will exist in each and every student. Be ready to identify in each student what seems to work best.

educational imperatives to remember

A number of educational principles apply to our teaching about the Bible with teens. These educational principles help to increase interest, and using them empowers the teacher personally, and the church incidentally, to involve youth in a keener and more personal way with the text of Scripture.

People learn best when they are involved, and we've already talked about the power of action learning. These principles will help get teens' attention so learning can begin. Getting attention increases involvement, so these educational principles cannot be omitted in the educational process of the church. Here are some statements that, if followed, increase the possibility of involvement in the learning exercise.

think about this. *Learning Truisms.* Review these and see how they relate to the study of God's Word.

( ) Principle #1: Things that are more meaningful are easier to learn.

( ) Principle #2: It is easier to learn when you are prepared.

( ) Principle #3: If directions are clear, it is easier to feel you have accomplished the task.

( ) Principle #4: People learn better when the presentation is exciting and novel.

( ) Principle #5: People learn better if the exercise if not too long.

( ) Principle #6: People learn better in friendly environments.

( ) Principle #7: Teens need variety in order to learn best.

How do these principles relate to teens and Bible study? Let me suggest some ways.

teach meaningful truth

What is the world like for teenagers? How does youth culture impact what they see as important? Answers to these questions impact the topics that need clarification in Bible study.

Teens growing up in the Millennial Generation, or Generation Y, is the second one that will grow up in a postmodern world. This world has lots of questions, but few, if any, answers. In this segmented world, teens long to be "connected to life."[2]

Walt Mueller in his engaging book about youth culture says, "As hope-filled ambassadors of Jesus Christ, we should be listening and responding with urgent compassion. Instead, those of us who have been given the task of leading the young to the soul-satisfying 'bread of life' (John 6:35) and 'streams of living water' (John 7:38) may have unknowingly locked the bread box and shut off the water valve through our inability or unwillingness to hear the nuances of their cries."[3]

In the Old Testament, God calls Moses to do a specific job for Him. He is to go back to his culture, one that put the Hebrews in positions of subservience and placed wealth and power in the hands of the elite. It was a culture that Moses knew best. He had lived insight into the inner working of Pharaoh's court and knew the decision making process of this pagan culture. God was wise selecting Moses—just the person for the job—solely aware of the culture that had trained him.

It is equally important for those of us who want to be missionaries to the youth to understand what is central to this "alien" culture. As adult church members, we've probably forgotten what we were like when we were young. We've forgotten the power of culture in framing our responses and sorting our priorities. We've forgotten how the music and films, TV and video games framed the context of our reality. And unless we can speak to the needs of the current culture, we probably will be seen only as one crying in the wilderness and unable to provide answers for the new questions the young are living with every day of their lives.

If the Bible provides "present truth" to this generation, then we must select carefully, seek relevance, and deal honestly and lovingly with the cultural tags that identify this culture itself. It is often said that if the church doesn't listen, they can't understand. As young people learn that they are not understood, the church becomes a place where they feel alien. Remember, in pastoral counseling jargon, "people often change and grow to the degree that they feel understood."

Again, Mueller provides help to us: "The cost of losing our ears is great. Whoever takes interest and listens with both ears will be given the privilege of influence." God's people are typically surprised not only to learn that our young are not listening to us, but who they are listening to."[4]

try this. *Culture Watch.* How well do you know your youth culture? Take a culture walk in your local mall looking for cultural characteristics and distinctiveness, including what values and beliefs, behaviors and problems you observe. See if you can answer these questions:
   1. What are the visible signs of youth culture?
   2. What are the sounds of youth culture?
   3. What are teens buying?
   4. What are the teens talking about?
   5. What books and magazines are they reading?

6. How do the geographic locations in which they live affect their values, beliefs, and behaviors?

Listening to the sounds of youth culture can prepare you with points of contact with your youth. If this is true, then time must be spent listening to the music of the times, watching some of the programs teens are consumed with, understanding the magazines they are reading, and above all, becoming intelligent in the technology that ties them together. To say it simply, if you don't text message, you are way too old!

You will discover that your young people are almost always more interested in studying what they want to study than in what you want to teach. So rise to this challenge to find our what turns your youth on as they study.

try this. *Get Your Degree in God Studies.* Connect your students to experiences that fulfill the faith fundamentals that they will need as they live their lives with God. Do this: Ask your students to outline the topics that they want to examine, and then work with them to explore those topics from a biblical point of view, with an emphasis on helping them meet Jesus. "Solid biblical teaching in the context of a variety of topics won't be a stretch; God has a great deal to say about practically any subject."5
Announce the topics to be studies which the young people have selected as your group's "Degree in God Studies." Have your teens make a graduation diploma once they have completed their studies of Bible topics they have selected.

make sure you are prepared

The next principle of learning that impacts Bible study is that of the need for preparation in your teaching of Scripture. All too often we take the proof-text approach to Bible learning. You have a question? I have a text! This simplistic method usually backfires as teens grow and begin to analyze their understandings of God and His ways in the world. Not all of the texts really say what we think they say. We forget context, biblical culture, textual variants, and authors' particularities—all things that make a better interpretation of biblical material possible.[5]

Preparation for Bible study requires that we have good tools at our disposal. Christians in the last century could do careful Bible study using only a concordance and their own Bible. Today there are many, many more Bible study tools and aids.

try this. *Bible Study Tools.* Use this checklist to see just how many of the modern study tools you have or have tried. If you score less than three, get busy and build your Bible study resource library so you can help others understand the biblical text.

- () A study Bible
- () A Bible concordance
- () A Bible dictionary
- () A Bible encyclopaedia
- () A Bible commentary
- () A Bible atlas

so, how do i get help?

Obviously, when you can't understand, you must look for help. Let me suggest some directions. Some Christians are afraid they will become dependent on reference tools, and because of this, they hesitate to use them. Some say piously, "All I need is the Bible." And this is true to some extent. But good reference tools help us get into our Bibles. Most of these books represent the long study of dedicated people who have gleaned insights they have received from the Lord via the Holy Spirit. Their study can enrich our own. Here are some suggestions.

1. Get a good study Bible. This is your very first task. Some of the Bibles you can choose are more useful for personal Bible study than others. A good Bible for study should have large enough print to see and read for long periods of time. It also needs to have paper thick enough to make notes in margins without the ink running through the paper to the next page. Large, wide margins are useful, too, because they give room for making personal notes. And make sure the Bible you pick has good cross-references. Your choice of Bible might be determined by your choice of reference books and commentaries.

A number of new Bibles focus on particular application of the text and even provide extra material that focus on this practical understanding. The NIV Life Application Bible is particularly like this. There are lots of these types of Bibles available. Some focus on youth, others on families and the like. These life applications Bibles begin where other study Bibles end because they help you live what you learn. They combine the benefits of a commentary, devotional, guidebook, atlas, and of course, contain the Bible text too. Their purpose is to give a greater understanding of the Word and show you how to live your faith in your daily walk with God.

The NIV Study Bible gives insight into the text by providing page notes, introductions and backgrounds to each of the biblical books, outlines, in-text charts and diagrams, center-column references, and a complete concordance which helps lead into the Bible's themes, events and theological points.

To find a good study Bible, go to a Bible bookstore and spend some time looking at what is available. You can do your research on the World Wide Web too. There are Bibles designed and targeted to various age groups, interests, and concerns. There are devotional Bibles, one-year Bibles which help you read during a complete year, and even a Bible that provides information about discipling. And if you are a church youth leader, there is a one-stop source for study groups called the Serendipity Bible. Each section has an "open, dig, and reflect" questions on selected Scripture to start group discussion.

check this out. *Christian Youth-Oriented Bible Study Web Resource Materials.* Here is a list of age-targeted Bible study helps I have found useful in building my own studies using the Web.

() *Teen Life Ministries.* <http://www.teenlifeministries.com/thefactory.htm>

() *Student Bible.* <http://www.studentlifebiblestudy.com/>

() *Bible Study Tips.* <http://christianteens.about.com/od/biblestudyresources/a/runningbibstudy.htm>

() *Parent's Guide to Teen Bible Studies.* <http://peopleoffaith.com/teen-bible-study.htm>

() *Cornerstone Connections Study Guides.* <http://cornerstoneconnections.adventist.org/>

() *Teen Study Bibles.* <http://www.christianbooksbibles.com/index.asp?PageAction=PRODSEARCH&txtSearch=teen+study+bible&btnSearch=GO&Page=1&gclid=CM_aj-f5nokCFRlmWAodgiJ7UQ>

() *Christian Bible Studies.* <http://www.christianitytoday.com/

biblestudies/>

8. *Hancock Center Young Adult Podcast Study.* <http://www.churchpodcast.net/hancock.html>

9. *Teen Bible Studies.* <http://yourlearninginfo.net/learning/3/BibleStudy/teenbiblestudy/Teen-Bible-Study.html>

10. *Pre-Teen Bible Studies, PowerPoints.* <http://www.ssnet.org/qrtrly/index.html>

2. *Discover the benefit of a good concordance of the Bible.* A concordance lists every word in the Bible and provides insight to the original languages used in the ancient texts. A computerized concordance is especially helpful if you have access to a personal computer. There are many of these programs available. The better ones will display every text containing a given term within a split second or less. Many also allow you to refer to the original language, comparing word for word, even if you haven't studied Greek or Hebrew.

3. *Find a good Bible dictionary and Bible encyclopedia.* It can help you understand the words used in your Bible. Most Bible dictionaries are very helpful, giving you the original meaning of the words and terms used in the text. Here you will read about the customs, traditions, geography and background of the Bible times. A Bible encyclopedia is an expanded Bible dictionary with longer articles that deal in greater detail with more subjects.

4. *Look for a good Bible commentary*, one that gives you insights into the original words of the Bible, a commentary that can help you with the context of a passage. A commentary is a collection of explanatory notes and interpretations of the text of the Bible. It is written with the purpose of exploring and interpreting the meaning by looking at the words used, the grammar and syntax, and the context of the passage. Commentaries can increase your understanding of the Bible. There are many available from your local religious book center. Spend some time with the commentary to see if it reflects a particular theological perspective. But I try to look at a commentary after I have studied the text for myself. And remember, many commentary writers have their own particular brand of interpretation. Some may not even believe that the Bible is God's Word. So read widely and carefully. Commentaries come in all sizes and price ranges and perspectives.

5. *Check out other resources such as The Bible Amplifier, a series of books which are designed to help your study through the Bible book by book.* Rather than offering interpretations of the text, its purpose is to help you explore the Word on your own, discovering answers and coming to a deeper understanding through careful, guided study. A number of denominations have helpful material in this format for you to explore.

provide clear directions

This principle of creative Bible study is where this list turns from the process of study to its methods. Involving youth in Bible study is the most successful when the task is clearly defined and illustrated. Since young people often feel uneasy about putting themselves on the line when they might look foolish, providing clear directions is crucial.

First, in order to increase their individual participation, try to provide all of the materials they will need to do careful study. For example, provide a copy of the Scripture under discussion. If you do, you will eliminate one more reason not to get involved. If they didn't bring their Bible, or they don't have a new translation, you solve this by providing all they need to think about the text.

Second, give them freedom to try to understand it themselves. Avoid the preaching approach where you give the answer and they simply agree or disagree. Avoid any approach to the verses of the Bible that fails to give them permission to think. Ask them to try to find something in the text that they believe God is trying to say to them or their church family. Giving them the option to share something they believe God is giving to others, makes it easier to respond. On the other hand, some of the young people will give a personal application of the text. Give them the freedom without judgment to state their feelings and insights.

Third, pool their observations. Find some way to collect their responses. If you use a white board or chalkboard, list in short sentences a summary of their decision about the text you have selected for study. Now, you can add your comments to the list. That way you don't act as a final authority, but you add your understanding of the text to theirs. As you do this, you will probably notice an important fact. Most of the answers are very close to your own understanding of the text. But the dynamic that has surfaced in this process is giving young people freedom to try to understand the text for themselves. This is a crucial skill if the Bible is to become their personal guide for life.

Since young people in the early and middle teens are in the faith stage where personalizing of their religious understandings is central, you can contribute to their own understanding and confidence in their ability to hear God through the text of Scripture.

make bible study creative and exciting

One necessary factor in helping the young get involved in Bible study is the necessity for the presentation to be both creative and exciting. Young people are exposed to the best and worst that the world has to offer. With the media, magazines, television, DVDs, iPods, iPads, MP3s, smartphones with e-mails, Internet and text messaging all vying for their attention and time, the brains of our youth are in constant electrical vibrancy. Christ's church must recognize this competition, and since many young people are at this time of their lives making decisions that alter their paths, the church must take its teaching of Scripture seriously. After all, there are only a few ways that God communicates to His people. Prayer and Bible study are two of the most central, and since this is the case, making sure that the presentations of God's will in the Bible are relevant and interesting is the challenge of the leaders in any youth programming.

Being both exciting and creative is nothing new to the Bible. When you study Scripture, you recognize that God so wanted His will to be made known, He tries every way imaginable to get it out. When you study the Old Testament prophets, you begin to realize how focused God was in telling the story of salvation. He leaves nothing to chance or misinterpretation. God uses all of the literary devices at His disposal to maximize the truth's impact in everyday life.

The message the prophet gives concerning the future of God's people is creative and exciting.

try this. *Study in God's Creativity.* The Prophet Jeremiah was given a task of telling the Children of Israel who lived in Jerusalem that the Babylonians were all too soon going to overrun their capital city. But God wanted them to not only get ready, He wanted them to understand His mission and love for them all at the same time. God comes to Jeremiah, this teen-age prophet, and gives personal illustrations that describe the character of God. Look at these texts and the illustration and try to understand what God is trying to say to His people. After reading the text, talk about the central meaning of the metaphors and experiences described in this Old Testament book. Try to draw some conclusions that help clarify your understanding of the pictures of God portrayed in these texts.

○ Jeremiah 13. Linen shorts. How does it show God's love?

○ Jeremiah 16. Don't marry. What does this show about God's character?

○ Jeremiah 18:9. The potter's house. What does this share about God's care for us?

○ Jeremiah 19. The broken jar. How does this show God's concern for us?

○ Jeremiah 24. Good and bad figs. What does God do for us?

○ Jeremiah 32. Buy land and hide the deed in the ground, only to dig it up later. What is the purpose of this story?

○ Jeremiah 31:33. What does this share about God relationship to His people?

If God can be so creative in trying to communicate His will to the world, surely we can try something exciting and creative while teaching the young about His desire for them in the world.

keep it short and real

This principle of Bible study for youth is particularly crucial. One key phrase all young people learn is "it's boring." Now, it really may not be boring, but in this fast-moving world, much is evaluated by the speed at which things get done. We have fast food, quick menus, fast cars, and when we wait nano seconds for an Internet connection; it seems like eternity. It is no wonder young people find church boring. Often church services have as many as 15 elements in the worship service. Most young adult pastors recognize that you need to keep everything simple and snappy.

While talking to a teen pastor in a large urban church that has over 400 young people each week at a Bible study, I asked him what his secret to careful, involved study of God's word. He explained it this way: "I think that what seems to work best is a quick, focused, pointed interaction with a Bible text or story, allowing the teens to use their own imagination in determining the meaning and making an attempt at a personal application." All this, he said, could be done in about 20 minutes. The key is not to use too large a portion of God's word, and the second key is to make sure that freedom is given to the young person to try out his or her ability to derive insight from the text for their personal life. Keeping it short and to the point seems to be important to young people. Long, drawn-out studies of doctrinal issues or historical positions often are tiresome for the young.

As the young people grow and ideology and theology become important, perhaps in their young adult years, longer, in-depth studies and discussions are often more fruitful. But while they are young, keeping it simple and focused is by far the best method.

try this. *Read in-between the lines.* Try to encourage teen Bible reading. Challenge your young people in church to find a translation of the Bible that they particularly like (i.e. *The Message Bible* is a good one for teens), then let them know that it is not how much you read that is important, but challenge them to read the whole Bible through in one year. There are many programs that are available to help.

I particularly like the translations I have put on my Smart Phone. The software is called MyBible. It gives me a portion of Scripture each day in the New International Version. I can select how much time I want to read, and how fast I want to finish. I can even spread the reading over two years. It keeps me up-to-date as to how far I am, and reminds me daily about the next passage. "Encourage young people to read through the Bible so they can begin to understand the overall story of God and what faith in Jesus is all about."[7]

If you can get the whole group of youth to do it together, you can prepare a weekly devotional to share in your youth meeting based on the portion of scripture your whole group is studying for themselves during the week.

learn better in friendly environments

If you list the top ten issues that impact the faith maturity and denominational loyalty of young people, one particular area surfaces to the top. Our research with teens argues that church climate is one of the most important issues that encourages these areas of spiritual growth.[8]

If you want your young people to get involved in the church, and specifically feel comfortable to explore the biblical record, the church must provide a place where they can feel safe, comfortable and experience a friendly environment

What is the purpose of Biblical study? This is a crucial question, and the answer presupposes a critique on the culture that pervades our world and even now our church life. Today's Christian culture is destroying Christianity, so says, Walt Mueller, an expert on Postmodernism. He says, "Today's Christian culture so resembles the world, that standing *contra mundum*—against the world, in opposition to its culture—would amount to standing against itself."[9] If this is true, most young people don't have a biblical worldview. Their reference points are secular. The world presses in and provides the entertainment, their leisure-time activities, and their meaning.

Bible study provides an alternative to the life that impacts them daily. Bible perspectives generate deep values out of which good decisions can be made and positive lifestyle choices can be lived. Research by George Barna shows how many in the church approach things from a biblical worldview. He says, "The research also points out that even in churches where the pastor has a biblical worldview, most of the congregants do not. More than six out of every seven congregants in the typical church do not share the biblical worldview of their pastor even when he or she has one."[10]

So if you want to increase the involvement of your youth in Bible study, make sure everyone in charge of the study is friendly, open to new ideas, and excited about the possibilities of learning something new from the Word of God.

variety, it helps them learn

There are all kinds of methods that can be used to open the word of Scripture to youth. Don't be satisfied by using only a few, try to add to your methods creative approaches that can help your young people apply the text to their lives. That means you can explore many different approaches to study.

try this. *Creative Bible Study.* Here is a list of creative approaches with a one-sentence description of the method. Use your skills as a leader or parent to encourage as many approaches as possible.

() *Bible Rewrite.* Have the young people take a parable of Jesus and rewrite it into a contemporary story that teaches the same lesson. (Can be done in groups).

() *Bible Drama.* Take a story in the Bible and create a five-minute drama and enact it for your group. Debrief the meaning of the story after it is presented.

() *Bible Slide Show.* Learn a story from the Bible using six separate still-life displays. Have the people in the audience covers their eyes until the next scene is enacted. As the actors freeze in place, ask everyone to uncover their eyes. The faster you do this the more dramatic it becomes. Talk about each story and try to find a modern application.

() *Artistic Bible.* Give everyone paper, art pens, magazines, scissors, paste, marking pens, and give groups of three teens a topic to depict as a poster. Then have the group leader explain what it means and what lesson can be learned from the poster art.

() *Bible Interview.* Ask a panel of "experts" in your church to explain various doctrines of the church and give why that doctrine is important to them. Make sure you provide the biblical resources to everyone after the discussion so they can study on their own.

() *The Quiet Bible.* Have young people enter a room and from that point on, they are not allowed to speak. Like people from another culture, have four or five students try to explain the Gospel from their Bibles using simple objects, hand motions, drawings, or pictures only without speaking. Have youth watching the presentations take notes, guessing the meaning of the varied illustrations. After all are finished, let everyone talk and see what they thought the Bible was saying about these topics.

◗ *Bible for Parents.* Have your young people pick a topic that they think their parents would like to hear and write a five minute sermon or talk using the Bible as about the only source. Ask the parents to come to a group meeting and have six or seven young people share their insights into these topics. Talk to the parents inbetween each presentation to see if they felt it was important and how they relate to it.

Don't be afraid to try creative ideas when it comes to teen Bible study. If you value youth involvement, you will have to become innovative and try some ideas that are unique. There are many resources that may help you, but the main issue you will have to face is to move out of the safety of the envelope of comfort that you are used to. Creative study implies variety, and variety means you can't just keep doing what you have been doing when it comes to Bible study.

the home is the last stand

After a review of some principles that increase involvement at your church in the area of Bible study, it is important to talk about the use of the Bible at home and in family life. If we were to ask the question of the home, what is the most important time that can be spent together, we probably would not say time spent in Bible study. However, without a family that models the importance of the biblical text in the every-day running of the home, youth will miss an opportunity to see real Christianity in action.

Family worship may be the only time that young people see their significant adults interact with the Word of God. In our research of over 24,000 young people, only eight percent (8%) had any daily family study. And only forty-eight percent (48%) spent time once a month or more outside of church in this important exercise. So modeling faith in the home implies modeling Bible study as well.

Since the home is the most important arena for passing on the faith, unless young people see their parents studying the Word of God and trying to apply its principles in their own contemporary world, there will be little that others can do to encourage this practice. In a way, the family's involvement in Bible study is the last frontier—the place where Christianity can be learned by involvement and example.

How do you make personal Bible study real in the lives of the youth of the church? This is a personal question and deserves a personal answer.

Here are some of my suggestions that just might help young people get personal with the Word of God. When you read the Bible, try to:

◊ Hear the voice of God like someone you love.

◊ Listen to God talk to you simply knowing He wants you to.

◊ Put your whole being into hearing God. Get comfortable (physical), think seriously about what the text says, (mental), always try to make a personal application (spiritual). This way the whole of your life is involved in hearing God.

◊ Listen to God without any preconceived notion of what you might hear. Listen as though it was for the first time.

◊ Find a way to listen to God during your day and apply what you have learned in Bible study to your real life.

chapter 7 / endnotes

1. See <http://teentouch.org/>forTeachers.asp accessed on 11/17/10 for help to teachers as they try to help teens learn using the various aspects of basic motivators, 1-5.
2. Walt Mueller, *Engaging the Soul of Youth Culture: Bridging Teen Worldviews and Christian Truth* (Downers Grove, IL: InterVarsity Press, 2006), 18-19.
3. Walt Mueller, *Engaging the Soul of Youth Culture*, 19.
4. Walt Mueller, *Engaging the Soul of Youth Culture*, 25.
5. See V. Bailey Gillespie, *Wise For Salvation: Making Bible Study Real* (Riverside, CA: Hancock Center Publications, 2011) for a detailed look at ways that Bible study can become personal and interesting for the whole family.
6. Rick Lawrence, ed., *Youth Ministry in the 21st Century: the Encyclopedia of Practical Ideas,* (Loveland, CO: Group 2006), 31.
7. Adapted from Rick Lawrence, *Youth Ministry in the 21st Century*, 109.
8. See V. Bailey Gillespie, *Ten Years Later: A Study of Two Generations.* The chapters on the home and church.
9. Walt Mueller, *Engaging the Soul of Youth Culture*, 138-139.
10. George Barna, "Only Half of Protestant Pastors Have a biblical Worldview," *The Barna Update*, <www.barna.org/FlexPage.aspx?PageCMD=Print>.

chapter 8

getting involved in compassionate caring

before we get specific about the possibilities for youth involvement in your local church life, we want to lay out some basic ideas that you can incorporate into your model of church that encourages active participation by young people. These ideas can help your church reevaluate the importance of ministry to young people as well as point you toward more practical actions that illustrate the ideas shared here.

When it comes to making a practical, hands-on, feet-on-the-ground application of the Kingdom of God, it might be said in one simple phrase — *It's all about others.*

One of your earliest Bible stories shared in church probably was the Good Samaritan. Jesus shared a beautiful concept in this short story. It teaches that when someone is in need, position, experience, training, attitudes, or race mean absolutely nothing. When people hurt, the citizen of God's Kingdom always, yes, always finds some way to help.

Helping others, however, is a two-way street. When we act for someone else, it has an impact on us. The impact is subtle, but nevertheless real. Researchers have long known that there is a positive correlation (relationship) between religious behaviors and many aspects of one's life and the life of the nearby community. On the positive side, religious practice through community involvement leads to greater generosity in charitable giving. And we know that religious people who were involved in helping others were at least 15% more likely to report having tender, concerned feelings toward the disadvantaged in general.

Religious practice benefits not only individuals, but also communities. We know, for example, that religiously active men and women are often more sensitive to others and more likely to serve and give to those in need, and more likely to be productive members of their local community. Researchers also have recognized the impact that regular church attendance and involvement in local congregational life has had on one's sense of happiness and well-being. And we know that happy people tend to be productive and law-abiding and also tend to learn well, thus having a positive impact on local society in general.

Religion significantly affects the level of a person's sense of purpose in life; this leads to more productivity and satisfaction on the job and a more caring approach to the world.

research insights. Among Christian young people in our own research, we have discovered that many are already involved in helping activities; in fact, more often than their parents or older church members.

() 30% said they spend 1-2 hours per week in helping friends and neighbors with problems they have.

() 24% spend between 3-5 hours with the same activities.

() Another 33% spend between 6 hours to more than 20 hours a week.

This seems like a lot of hours helping others, but this research was for high school students only, and shows how involved young people already are in the lives of others. Many schools require these kinds of activities, and even some universities include service learning in their curricula. This is real evidence that student involvement is vital in the task of making this world more user-friendly.

why serve?

In asking young people why they volunteer, Christian young people provide some strong motivation, both biblical and personal, as to their 10 top reasons to volunteer.

Here are their answers in order of importance:

#1 — To broaden my personal experience (51%)

#2 — To do something worthwhile for others ((51%)

#3 — An important response to God's act of salvation (38%)

#4 — Volunteering made me feel needed (38%)

#5 — I wanted to serve my community (35%)

#6 — Doing it gives me a sense of personal satisfaction (35%)

#7 — To enrich my own spiritual life (35%)

#8 — I have a deep concern for those less fortunate (34%)

#9 — It gives me leadership opportunities (34%)

#10 — It fulfills my inner sense of interest in others (33%)

what motivates you?

As you can see, motivation for compassion towards others is complex. But one thing we know for sure is that churches and communities that encourage a family-like climate, that engage in challenging decision making and critical thinking, that are friendly and caring with a sense of deep spirituality through the communities' actions and spiritual practice, that respect diversity and encourage creative worship can expect their young people to be more active, attached to the church, and growing in their own religious lives. Add to this the important need for personal involvement in mission and community service, and you build a complete package for active involvement and growth.[1]

The problem is, however, not all church communities hold these values to be central. Instead, they can be critical of youth's attitudes, music, activities, restlessness, or boredom in relation to church life. What is missing is for the church to provide events, activities, actions that fully represent Christ and His mission on earth. Youth need involvement that teaches important lessons and provides experiences that are both educational and spiritual. In short, as Wayne French summarizes his research in his seminal book, *Creating Memories for Teens*, he identifies the benefits of youth involvement in activities that hold deep meaning and become "memory events." His list includes the following:

() Memory events have a life-long impact

() Memory events are a platform for personal spiritual impact

() Memory events develop genuine friendships

() Memory events develop a sense of belonging

() Memory events help adolescents feel valued

() Memory events bond adolescents to the church.[2]

Whatever the church can do to help young people think about the "big issues" in life — God, home, church, career, purpose, belonging, etc.— moves them toward spiritual maturity. The church can be an important place where these connections happen. The power of events and compassion lived out in actual involvement with others in need creates an event that is fixed in the memory in a clear way. And in the midst of youth growth, school activities, and parental demands, any opportunity the church can take to assist the young to reflect on their purpose in life and the meaning of the mission of God is a fruitful venture. Youth ministry professional Chap Clark from Fuller Theological Seminary makes a relevant point,

> "The power of memory as translated into story is what gives us the categories for how we live our lives. Especially with adolescents, who are in the midst of wild changes as they grow into adults, the memories they carry will form the basis of how they see themselves, their family and friends, and their God."[3]

is context important?

There is one simple constant in our lives that governs most of the ways we learn. Whether you are 12 or 65, there is something basic and powerful about doing something in a different context from what is our usual *modus operandi*. It may be Sunday morning at the local children's hospital, or a weekend outing with family or close friends, a short-term mission assignment in Mexico at an orphanage, or a week in Kenya at a game preserve/mission school serving children affected by health issues and in need of Christian education. Mission trips, community service stints, helping someone in need offer opportunities to deepen our understanding of life and purpose. Being involved reveals just how small our world really is while the world's needs are often overwhelming.

try this. *Pace your mission trip.* "Most youth workers tend to think of a mission trip in a single phrase: the trip. *New* research suggests we need to expand our view of trips into three time phases:

before the trip, *during* the trip, and *after* the trip."[4]

Before the trip — ask young people what they expect to get out of the experience. Have them write a notebook five things they would like to learn, feel, experience, or try.

During the trip — Try to have a debriefing each evening asking young people to share their experiences as to what they learned, how they felt, and what new thing they have experienced.

After the trip — Have them write a short story about something that happened to them on the trip. Tell them it can be a secular story or can reflect a religious theme.

Finally in the closing discussion, spend time asking if the mission experience met their expectations in a personal way and if they would like to share it. Try to get an appointment with the adults of the church during a worship service for some youth to share their experiences and how serving others helped change their viewpoint.

So when it comes to understand teen motivation for mission, try to help young people capture the big picture.

() Ask questions that help clarify their reasons for doing acts of kindness.

() Review the life of Jesus and his constant concern for the care of the oppressed.

() Remind them of the Old Testament Prophets who decried the *status quo* and stretched the minds of the people to think beyond themselves and their wants to the needs of the community and to those less fortunate—widows, elderly, poor, needy, and the disenfranchised.

clarifying mission and message

Share the facts about community volunteering and service. For students it is all good news! It seems that adults who began serving as youth were more than twice as likely to serve later on as adults. Students engaged in service learning indicated an increase in the way they viewed their community's needs and truly believed that they could make a difference in this world. And of particular interest to students and teachers is the fact that those involved in service learning activities during their school years improved their grade point average (GPA) from a "B" to a "B+" as they became

144

more active in caring for others. Involvement in service and compassionate care for others increased the resiliency to involvement in at-risk behaviors and lowered the arrest record of school-age young people too. So the good news outshines anything bad about caring for others.

The testimonies from Wayne French's research again offers clear, positive proof of those who have served.

"...My work with a soup kitchen in my church provided me with so many opportunities to talk about what Jesus was really like. The smiles on the faces of those we helped just can't be wiped from my memory. And, personally, I think I understand a bit better the passion of Jesus as he looked on His world and wondered if anyone ever caught a true glimpse of His father. To be a part of that message makes me very humble."

"...Definitely the STORM Co. Trip....We did kid's club at the Aboriginal Mission, which included singing, crafts, sports, face painting, ballooning and clowning. For our community project, which was done at the state school, we rebuilt the sand pit, redid their flower gardens and installed irrigators. We also did some minor paint repair to the water tank at the community centre. It was hard manual labour but the thought of the joy it would bring to the kids and community made it all worthwhile."

"This trip made me realize that there are so many people in the world that are living in worse-off conditions who when they are told about God fully appreciate it. I now realize that our problems are so small. The tiniest bit of help is so appreciated. I can see that God is working and He is real."[5]

a biblical rationale

I have waited to the end of this chapter to share what the Bible says about helping others. Feel free to use this material in your own Bible study or with your teen group. In searching the many texts in the Old and New Testament regarding service to others, I realized only a few could frame the basis for a clear theology of compassionate care. What would be my choice of biblical passages to share with teens? My best are below.

try this. *Six Verse Theology.* Read in small groups (3-5 people) the following texts and ask your youth to build a theology (What does God think?) of caring and compassion. Post your outline of what the Bible says about this topic on poster paper, then share each group's ideas about what is important to remember about this topic.

1. *Luke 6:38* — *"Give, and it will be given to you. A good measure, pressed down, shaken together and running over, will be poured into your lap. For with the measure you use, it will be measured to you."*

2. Hebrews 13:16 — *"Do not neglect to do good and to share what you have, for such sacrifices are pleasing to God."*

3. 1 John 3:17 — *"But if anyone has the world's goods and sees his brother in need, yet closes his heart against him, how does God's love abide in him?"*

4. Matthew 25:35-40 — *"Then the King will say to those on his right, 'Enter, you who are blessed by my Father! Take what's coming to you in this kingdom. It's been ready for you since the world's foundation. And here's why:*

> *I was hungry and you fed me,*
> *I was thirsty and you gave me a drink,*
> *I was homeless and you gave me a room,*
> *I was shivering and you gave me clothes,*
> *I was sick and you stopped to visit,*
> *I was in prison and you came to me.'*

"Then those 'sheep' are going to say, 'Master, what are you talking about? When did we ever see you hungry and feed you, thirsty and give you a drink? And when did we ever see you sick or in prison and come to you?' Then the King will say, 'I'm telling the solemn truth: Whenever you did one of these things to someone overlooked or ignored, that was me—you did it to me.'"

5. Acts 4:32-35 — *"All the believers were one in heart and mind. No one claimed that any of their possessions was their own, but they shared everything they had. With great power the apostles continued to testify to the resurrection of the Lord Jesus. And God's grace was so powerfully at work in them all that there were no needy persons among them. For from time to time those who owned land or houses sold them, brought the money from the sales and put it at the apostles' feet, and it was distributed to anyone who had need."*

6. 1 Timothy 6:17-19 — *"Command those who are rich in this present world not to be arrogant nor to put their hope in wealth, which is so uncertain, but to put their hope in God, who richly provides us with everything*

so now what can you do?

The reasons for volunteering are as individual as you are, but no matter what your reasons, you can get a lot out of trying. And as you help others, you help yourself. One of the hardest things to do is to find a caring situation that truly fits your personality and one that is consistent with your understanding of the message of Jesus in your own life. Here are 20 ways for teens to help others by volunteering. As a youth professional you might use this list as a check sheet to see what your own youth group might be interested in, or it can be done personally to see what kind of experiences you need to organize so the majority of your youth can get committed and involved.

1. Serve at a homeless shelter
2. Serve at a food bank, or begin one yourself
3. Near a big medical center, try volunteering there or at the Ronald McDonald house next door.
4. Are there any Special Olympics nearby?
5. Build a house with Habitat for Humanities
6. Volunteer at a state or regional park
7. Check out your city's mayor's office; see if you can help
8. Libraries often need free help, or even reading to children
9. How about a senior center near your church
10. Animal shelter? Those pets need care too
11. The United Way is always looking for assistance
12. The Salvation Army, Red Cross
13. Environmental organizations. Check out Project Learning Tree, http://www.plt.org, and see what they might have for you to do
14. Help around the church with the yard work
15. How about your neighbors? Anyone need special help?
16. Holiday helping — Thanksgiving, Christmas, etc., people need special help during these holiday times
17. Political Campaigns. During election years they always need helpers
18. Start a help phone line, or volunteer for one in your community
19. How does your church need help? There must be chil-

dren's groups, elderly groups, or functions you can help assist

20. Use your own imagination....think, create, act and then share what happened with others so they can be encouraged

thinking about doing, or just doing

The challenge is not in finding things to do or thinking about what we might do; the challenge for any youth group is to actually get going doing something.

I know of one young adult ministry which is a part of a large institutional church. They felt that God's call to service was crucial if they were going to be a Christ-centered community of faith within the umbrella of the larger church. Looking around they felt that the larger part of the church was involved in their own ministries, personal and public, but their age group was not. Something had to happen if God was to be blessed in their community. They decided to open a thrift store. They named it after their own branding, identified to the community as a part of the large church outreach and began to collect things. And collect things is now an understatement. They have expanded to a large warehouse, need now to expand to another one, do almost $500/day of sales of donated goods which they sell for as little as $1.00/item. They have found hundreds of needy families to serve and the ministry funds itself now, has full-time workers that take a small stipend for helping, uses hundreds of local church members as volunteers, and God seems to be richly blessing this small band of believers who wanted to do great things for good with God.

There are other stories of how God has blessed churches, youth groups, families, and youth themselves by stretching beyond their own needs to focus on someone else in need. Somehow, whe you give of yourself to others you learn something unique about the ministry of Jesus. This is the message of Jesus in action. The reason we live the message of Jesus is because he lived the nature of God.

The Apostle Paul said it in another way in his letter to the Corinthians. He said, *"This service that you perform is not only supplying the needs of the Lord's people but is also overflowing in many expressions of thanks to God"*[6]

living large today

Many today think that the age we live in is now post-Christian. When you look around you almost can believe it, because Christianity is often attacked as irrelevant to today's life or is just not taken seriously by most of society. It seems that Christianity has almost been pushed off the court, so to speak, outside the foul lines of culture. There are a number of responses to this possible truth that have been suggested. One might be to just get mad, stomp you feet, or even throw something. We might shout to whoever might listen, "Hey....Yeah, you, over there, Listen to me. We Christians have something very important for you to hear." A more usual response, however, is to simply hide. After all, it is "us" versus "them." Our response could be to sit on our truth and just watch prophecy be fulfilled as the world goes down and down.

But if you truly think about these two responses, they don't honor God or the Gospel. God simply calls us to service, compassionate, loving, selfless, and inclusive. That is what Jesus wants, I believe. But in a post-Christian world, how are our friends, associates, classmates, neighbors, girls and boys ever going to know something about the loving God that gave His life for us? Look at what the Bible says: *"No one has ever seen God; but if we love each other, God lives in us and his love is made complete in us."* (1 John 4:12) God is seen through the lives of his children and followers. People cannot see God, but they can see us. Loving others as God loved them is our challenge.

Research on religious experience shares that most people make decisions about life-changing attitudes, values, and commitments because of someone else's influence on their lives—teachers, pastors, friends, family. The strongest argument for Jesus Christ God has in the world is His life on display in His people, you and me. That is why service to others is not only important, but central to the Gospel and to our understanding of what God is truly like.

chapter 8 / endnotes

1. Roger Dudley, *Why Our Teenagers Leave the Church: Personal Stories from a 10-year Study* (Hagerstown, MD: Review and Herald Publishing Association, 2000), 197-199.
2. Wayne French, *Creating Memories for Teens* (Warburton, Victoria: Signs Publishing Company, 2005), 30-31.
3. Quoted in Ibid., vii.
4. Chap Clark & Kara E. Powell, *Deep Ministry in a Shallow World* (Grand Rapids, MI: Zondervan, 2006), 9.1.
5. Quotations regarding the positive way in which service is seen in the young are recorded in part in Wayne French, *Creating Memories for Teens.*
6. 2 Corinthians 9:12 (Message Bible).

chapter 9

getting involved in church life

here is an interesting observation about the state of young people and their concerns. It serves as a concluding portrait that we can identify with and just might see in some of the young people we know, love, and serve.

> "Hey, boomers, Xers: Hold on to your baseball caps. There is a new generation upon us, the oldest barely out of high school, the youngest not yet born. They're not just any crop of youngsters, either. These are our own little heirs and scions: brilliant, gorgeous, practically perfect. You can brag all you want that they're chips off the old block, but they are not. They may have been smitten by Furbys and American Girl dolls and 'N Sync the same way the boomers took to coonskin caps, Barbie, and the Beatles. But they were weaned on everything from the Internet and prosperity to academic pressure cookers, Columbine, working moms, and high divorce rates. They are fundamentally different in outlook and ambition from any group of kids in the past 50 to 60 years. The differences between us and them are not insignificant or academic, because the wave that is approaching is very big, nearly as big as the baby-boom generation. It is clear from talking to them that they already know they don't want to live or work the way we do."[1]

getting involved in church life

There is no question about that fact that today's youth have a personal agenda and many young people who become active in the church reflect adult's highest hopes and possible dreams as well as all-to-often their most gripping fears. Due to this dichotomy and the culture's general understanding about teens, it is not always easy to share a 1-2-3-step solution for their involvement in church life. After all, in this process of attachment, there are detractors at work. Young people get involved in school activities that absent them from regular involvement, and even parents, who struggle themselves with regular commitment, impact youth's decisions for consistent participation in a youth group or in church life itself. Add to this the fact that both the church and the young person's religious commitment are varied and inconsistent in their representation in real life, and you feel the evident tension.

Research on the spiritual and religious life of adolescents provides some help in this area. There is a huge array of early research in the sociology and psychology of religion regarding religious attitudes in the United States. In reviewing this research, you notice it generally targets young adults between the ages of 18 and 25. Those studying younger adolescent religion and teens seem few and far between, but lately, more attention has been given American adolescents between the ages of 10 and 19, a group representing about 14% of the total population of the United States.[2]

Teens and preteens are the age group where most churches should target change. Thus, it is important to recognize that insights into the research done with this age group that observes their religious life can enhance the local churches' awareness of their spiritual needs and provide insight into their faith practice. In addition, parents and church workers who see their ministry for youth as important can learn and appropriately respond to these findings.

Using this research as a window through which to observe and assess American religion in young people as a whole, we glimpse the religious diversity we daily experience in local congregations. A variety of recent studies have made diverse claims about the character and transformation of American religion, according to Christian Smith in her comprehensive book, *Soul Searching: The Religious and Spiritual Lives of American Teenagers*.[3] These insights can inform us as we try to involve young people in church life.

some troubling research insights

Here is a summary of recent research on Adolescence and Religion with a sample of their primary sources and some obvious observations about their findings. You will notice that some of these findings are are up for multiple interpretation, however their insights provide an interesting insight for conversations about the centrality of the church for young people.

() The diversity of the American adolescent religious experience is demonstrated with its influx of new immigrants who expand the demographic pluralism of American faiths.[4] By 2050 the latest census survey in the USA suggests that Hispanics will make up the majority of the United States population. However in reality, immigrant populations are an extreme minority in most congregations as they tend to separate culturally into their own congregations which creates the challenge of providing cultural-specific ministry in many local churches.

() The impact of consumerism, individualism, and subjectivity impacting religious "seekers" contributes to the personalization and uniqueness of religious life.[5] This research finding regarding seekers may be overrated. There are few "spiritual" seekers in any given congregation and while the youth culture and popular culture impacts teens, they reflect the general population in this arena. Not everyone becomes a "seeker."

() Other researchers make the claim that young people are becoming more and more estranged from their traditional religious upbringing. In its place, they are opting out for a more postmodern and individualistic faith experience.[6] This finding seems to be an overstatement. On the other hand, other recent research indicates that teens are very attached to their own traditions and the overwhelming majority of them are pleased to attend their parents' church as they grow. This is true of the *Valuegenesis* research as well.

() Along the same lines, other research shares that American religion is generally losing its coherence caused by historical religious traditions, and as individuals they are eclectically mixing and matching their own spiritual practices to other diverse faith traditions.[7] Again, this does not seem to be particularly true. Teens seem committed to their own church and if given the chance, claim they would like to become more involved.

() Still, some research suggests that youth are marginalizing religion in their lives and not making practical transitions from their belief to their actual lives.[8] Teens seem, on the contrary, to be active in their faith, even more so than are their parents. Christian young people regularly participate in church attendance, personal prayer life, community outreach, and beliefs in a significant manner.

◊ In contrast to these, others see young people moving back to traditional beliefs and practices along with historical orthodoxy. This is seen in its positive aspect by denominational religions.[9] It is true that hurches have never meant more than they do now to young people in local congregations.

In the National Study of Youth and Religion, we learn more generational insights. And, much like our *Valuegenesis* research done with two separate decades of churched young people, we discover that most of the accounts of adolescent religion are shared in distinctly generational terms which suggests that "American baby boomers first opened the door to profound religious changes and that younger generations now drive the cutting edge of fundamental religious transformation in America."[10]

You can see why involving young people in your church life is crucial.

In looking at the *Valuegenesis* research project that frames the basis of our own denominational research results and comparing them with the National Study mentioned above, we see obvious overlaps and agreements that relate to our understanding of young people and clarify some of the misconceptions above found in some research studies. So to save you time and effort, let me provide you with a short list of insights that seem to make a real difference as you attempt to involve the young people of your congregation and family into the active, faith life of your local church. How your local church answer them"

insight no. 1. where is the relevance?

What seems to be the challenge for the church is not getting youth interested in attendance and participation, but rather making sure that their religious experience is personal. The church must also communicate that it cares about reviewing the landscape of their personal religious convictions. So, heightening their interest is not the challenge. It seems they are very interested in religion; in fact, statistically over three-fourths of those studied in most major religious studies claim the basic importance of religion in their lives.

What is the problem then? The insights into teen's religious lives are most interesting. In fact, "huge numbers of U.S. teenagers are currently in congregations, feel okay about them, mostly plan to continue to stay involved at some level, and generally feel fine about the adults in their congregations. But the congregations simply do not mean that much or make much sense to many of them."[11] Since young people seem to be happy to be a part of the congregations they grew up into, and they basically seem pleased about them, the challenge in the local church and family is to find ways to make this faith commitment more active and central in their lives. Church life must become relevant and realistic. The challenge for change then is on the local congregation to allow the church practice—worship, prayer, actions—to meet the specific and unique needs of the young in the congregation. Making the church relevant to youth is a noble cause, but to do so takes thought and refocus for many churches.

try this. *Church Clay Figures.* Get a group of teens and their parents together for a focus group about the church and young people. Get a group of about 10 teens and their parents, then try this to jump-start your focus group's discussion about the challenge of being a relevant church to its youth.

Some people are less verbal than others so they might need a little help. This activity helps you along this path. Making clay figures helps people who are less verbal to express themselves.

Give each person in the group a lump of clay and a topic to sculpt. Good topics involve some kind of self-perception: How do you think people see this church? How do you want it to be seen? What do you want it to grow into?

The expressions can be portraits, symbols, or metaphors. For example, a "big hand" might represent community involvement, a broken coffee mug might represent being a broken vessel in need of grace, etc. You'll need modeling clay, Play-Dough, or Silly Putty to make this work.

Share your creations together, see what the images bring to

others minds and then talk about the meaning of the church in your own life as a leader of young teens or young adults.

insight no. 2. what happened to creativity?

Growing churches have lots of programming. Often families incorporate religious practice in the same manner. Repeating programs and practice over and over again does not guarantee significance. And this is the problem. Just as young people's religious life reflects variety, the church life that invites participation must be varied and creative. We get into ruts in religion. Tradition takes hold and becomes ritual. But just because we've always done it "that" way does not warrant continued repetition or justify its importance. So if your church wants to increase participation and involvement, this desire must be coupled with creative planning.

In business, this is called "thinking outside of the box." Corporate America challenges its employees to think in divergent ways to increase productivity. In religion, doing so is sometimes called heresy! But, of course, that in most cases isn't quite true. Being creative heightens interest and increasing interest helps learning and, of course, learning (knowledge) is one central aspect of religious growth.

Thinking outside the box simply means trying to be sensitive to the working of the Holy Spirit as we understand new ways to see God's truth and presence in this world. Theologically speaking, we might say that creativity is another aspect of the work of the Holy Spirit in the life of the church. We believe that God communicates with His children through a number of ways—nature, impression, Scripture, and through the person and life of Jesus Christ. The Spirit of God in some ways functions like a verb in a sentence. It is the action word of God. The Spirit convicts, crystallizes, firms, directs, moves, and quickens (to use a biblical term). Because of this action of God in the world, as we try to find new ways to express the central truths of God or creative ways to explore the revelation of God in nature or in the Word, we are in touch with God through His Spirit.

When you think of your local church programming for young people, remember that being creative is a positive experience for the young. They are learning about God, and they don't have the history that adults have. And they are not committed to looking at only one answer to difficult questions or challenges. Being creative can heighten attention and encourage commitment and involvement.

try this. *How many ways can you use a brick?* Take a regular brick and put it in the front of the room. Give everyone a 3x5 index card and pencil. Ask this question: "How many ways can you use a brick?" Jot down in a short sentence as many ways as possible. The most creative people will be able to list as many as 12 to 15 ways. Some people will stop at six or seven. Then take a religious topic such as: How can we learn about God's Love," or "How can the Sabbath rest be realized in our busy world?" and see how creative your youth group can be. Divergent thinking often enriches such religious practices as worship style, understanding of the metaphors of the Bible, or understanding biblical truths and makes them real to the believers.

The Bible is filled with creative approaches to learning. Jesus used parables, metaphors, illustrations, object lessons, preaching, questions, action, and experiences in order to teach about His Kingdom. He was not alone in the use of these creative methods. Take, for example, the Old Testament Prophets and their mission to challenge God's people to become socially sensitive and remember their calling as the chosen of God. The Psalmist challenges believers to "remember the lilies of the field, how they grow." A simple statement, but profound as well. Now we have to consider them. How do they grow? Who cares for them? And through careful reflection, we see God's concern for each of us. Jeremiah wore an ox yoke as an example of God's teamwork, and Ezekiel cooked a burned meal to show how much might happen to them if they forgot His power and love. So take time to try something exciting and be as creative as the God-given gift to you allows.

insight no. 3. where are all the parents?

Common wisdom suggests that as teens grow older, they move away from their parents' beliefs and values for a period of time. One of the more popular stereotypes of young faith is that they are religious dissidents, "who find their parents' religious beliefs and practices old and meaningless and want to have little to do with any of it." While this may be true for some, the vast majority of American teenagers grow to be reflectors of their parents faith and practice.[12] We have already hinted at the centrality of religious parenting and its power to impact the faith decisions of their children. So it goes without saying that the spiritual modeling of the parental mentors is crucial. Ask yourself some central questions: "What does my religious life teach my children about what God is like?" "How does my church attendance model what I hope for my children when they are adults?" "Are my attitudes and actions representative of a clear understanding of what God expects from His followers?" The power of a parent's modeling faith is strikingly evident in the findings of Merton Strommen in his book, *Passing On The Faith,* where he shares a research finding that states that, "religious practices in the home virtually double the probability of a congregation's youth entering into the life and mission of Christ's church."[13]

By extension, we see the church as a type of parent to the youth of the church. What does this relationship teach the young? Do the youth of your church see adults working together, or is there disagreement in the church over worship practice or church music? Do the young have clear models of Christlike relationships? Have the youth ever seen arguing, contention, and political maneuvering? Most churches could not have entirely positive responses to these questions. After all, the church is a human institution trying to reflect the Kingdom of God. It will not always be what it might become. Nevertheless, young people must see in the lives of their parents and church parents as close a model of Christ that as possible.

If you want you young people involved in the church, they have to see a place that is positive and accepting.

try this. *Interview your membership.* Take the following survey after a worship service at your church. Have four or five teenagers talk to about 20 church members to see how they feel about their church. Here are some of the questions you might ask.

Why did you come to our church the first time?

How many times do you attend during a month?

Are you a first, second, or third (or more) generation member?

insight no. 4. what methods are crucial?

If we want involvement, we suggested that you must use methods that heighten involvement and insight. Adding to this observation, I want to review how to teach young people to ensure that the meaning of the learning experience is understood. There are many ways to ensure a deeper learning experience. First, we must be intentional in what we teach. Be clear on this point. It is important for the church and for the home to teach both what is wanted and what is needed. All too often we yield only to the prior issue. We ask teens what they want, and we become so busy trying to please them, we forget that the learning universe is larger than our desires.

If you want to learn to be an archeologist, you must master the vocabulary, study history, learn methods, and at some time spend weeks in an archeological square sifting through the dirt. The learning is not just telling: it is sharing, experiencing, thinking and reflection. Here is a learning model that might be helpful as you spend time teaching young people about God's will for their lives and the life and thought of your church.

John Losey, director of Praxis training programs, suggests a simple modified learning cycle that we can apply to religious understanding. He calls it the Amazing Learning Loop of Depth as a model that might give a practical sequence of events that build toward real learning and meaning.[14] This learning loop has four steps. (1) *Inform*—here the content of what needs to be learned is explored and might include skills, attitudes and perspectives. (2) *Apply*—after clarifying, the new information must be applied to real life if it is ever going to make sense. (3) *Reflect*—After it is applied, time must be spent to allow the experience to sink in. The amount of time you allow to this step in the learning process will make a great deal of difference and impact the next phase of the learning loop. (4) *Re-view*—Here the learning is refined and t he information is tested as to relevance and insights into changes that need to be made. And the learning loop is back to inform as new information that is discovered in the re-view process is applied, reflected on and reviewed again.

This process uses an important psychological truth. Repetition, and repetition well done, makes learning stick.

In practice this is much like any other learning loop. such as Larry Richard's *Look, Book,* and *Took* model—a model used for teaching scripture that begins with a story or illustration *(Look),* then moves to searching the Bible for answers *(Book),* and finally seeks to answer the question of "so what" as you make an application of the biblical message *(Took).* Most religious learning loops give young people a chance to apply the information you have provided them and to move them dynamically to the next step in understanding. By reflection and review you move them to be concerned and to understand what they have learned. Each step prepares you for the next. So in your planning for the youth of your church, try to implement some type of feedback and reflection in order for the application to make sense.

We are responsible as Christians to be dependent on the power of God to help us, but with that dependence is the responsibility to teach well. We should try to teach to the best of our ability and recognize that the fruits of the Spirit are God's responsibility. We must control what we can. So using the best learning experiences as possible will help us bring Glory to God.[15]

insight no. 5. is there love in your church?

We cannot conclude this book without recognizing important findings about congregations that make them user-friendly for the youth and young adults. Our research identifies a number of attributes that build a rich congregational life that makes a difference in the faith maturity and faith life of the young in its midst. We call them "Positive Influences," but they are simply factors that make a congregation the best possible place for young Christians to grow. Early research called "The Effective Christian Education Study" sponsored by Search Institute found that the degree that congregations welcome strangers was one important factor in building a congregational family. They identified a hospitable environment as important in accomplishing this task.[16]

In the *Valuegenesis* research completed in 2000 and now in 2010 by the Seventh-day Adventist church, we discovered the following positive influences that make a difference in the attitudes of the young people in the areas of faith maturity and denominational loyalty:

() *Congregational Climate*—Whether or not the church was seen as warm, open, and accepting in nature, and if it provided an open, challenging,and thought-provoking environment in which to grow towards God.

() *Local Ministry Excellence*—Many of the activities of the local church fall into this rubric: Providing interesting programs for young people that are intergenerational in nature (involve children, youth, and young adults on a regular basis), churches that build thought-provoking and challenging critical thinking programming that focuses on discussions about central issues in the church as youth build an ideology and theology.

() *Congregational Support*—Such influences as the experience of being nurtured by caring peers and adults and being exposed to religious educational programs and leaders who are supportive and compassionate are crucial if maturity of faith and loyalty are to be the result.

() *Uplifting Worship Experiences*—Building relevant, inspirational, and age-appropriate worship environments is important if involvement is a goal.

() *Building a Grace Orientation*—This is not a complex term; it reflects the action of God in our salvation and the attitudes we express as we live a Christian life. Churches that reflect this orientation move the Kingdom of God to reality in the lives of the young.[17]

what can you expect your church to do?

Every church, large or small, urban or suburban, rich or poor can make some changes. Change is a principle of Christian living. Change can be all-encompassing or infinitesimal, movement is essential. Some may be able to reorient their programming along creative lines; others just might become relational congregations where building friendships with young people is central.

In *Big Questions, Worthy Dreams,* Sharon Parks looks at the twenty-something years and shares what she thinks must be done to involve and engage young adults in the issues of the church and world. She suggests building "mentoring communities." She defines them as being characterized by an "intentional, mutually demanding, and meaningful relationship between two individuals, a young adult and an older, wiser figure who assists the younger person in learning the ways of life."[18] She challenges congregations to take these connections through relationships seriously and recognize their power in religious formation. This is good counsel for every local congregation as they reorder their priorities for ministry to the young. So take to heart the challenge to encourage your church to become a caring one. And begin. . .yes, begin to do something to make general changes and get young people involved in an active church that is living the Kingdom of God in a very real and practical way.

chapter 9 / endnotes

1. Brian O'Reilly, *Fortune*, Monday, July 24, 2000).
2. Studies directed towards information regarding teen religion now include the *Valuegenesis* Studies 1, 2, and 3. This research on faith, values, and commitment is part of the on-going work to enlighten the Seventh-day Adventist church as to the religious formation of the young people grades six through twelve and to clarify the roles of the home, church, and religious school in faith growth. This research, which began in 1990 still continues to this day. Couple this research with that done in the *National Study of Youth and Religion* conducted from 2001 to 2005 at the University of North Carolina at Chapel Hill and you have a rather complete look at churched and non-churched preteens and teenagers.
3. Christian Smith with Melinda Lundquist Denton, *Soul Searching: The Religious and Spiritual Lives of American Teenagers*, (New York, NY: Oxford University Press, 2005), 5.
4. Diana Eck, *A New Religious America: How a "Christian Country Has Become the World's Most Religiously Diverse Nation* (New York, NY: HarperCollins, 2001).
5. See, for example, Wade Clark Roof, *Spiritual Marketplace: Baby Boomers and the Remaking of American Religion* (Princeton, NJ: Princeton University Press, 1999); Wade Clark Roof, *A Generation of Seekers: The Spiritual Journeys of the Baby Boom Generation* (New York, NY: HarperCollins, 1993)
6. Tom Beaudoin, *Virtual Faith: The Irreverent Spiritual Quest of Generation X* (San Francisco, CA: Jossey-Bass, 1998); Steve Rabey, *In Search of Authentic Faith: How Emerging Generations Are Transforming the Church* (Colorado Spring, CO: Waterbrook Press, 2001).
7. Robert Fuller, *Spiritual But Not Religious* (New York, NY: Oxford University Press, 2001); Lynn Schofield Clark, *From Angels to Aliens:*

Teenagers, the Media, and the Supernatural (New York, NY: Oxford University Press, 2003).

8. See this discussion in Patricia Hersch, *A Tribe Apart: A Journey into the Heart of American Adolescence* (New York, NY: Ballantine Books, 1998).

9. See *Valuegenesis* research, V. Bailey Gillespie and Michael J. Donahue. *Ten Years Later* supports this movement, as does Coleen Carroll, *The New Faithful: Why Young Adults are Embracing Christian Orthodoxy* (Chicago, CA: Loyola Press, 2002).

10. Christian Smith, *Soul Searching*, 5.

11. Christian Smith, *Soul Searching*, 266,

12. *The National Survey of Youth and Religion*, 2002-2003, reports percentages regarding beliefs held that are similar to their mothers' and fathers'. 41% of religious teens say their religious beliefs are "very similar" to their mothers', and 36% say the same about their fathers' beliefs. These statistics, when coupled with the next category of response, show an ever greater acceptance of parental beliefs. For example, 37% of the teens say their beliefs are "somewhat similar" to their mothers', and 36% say their beliefs are "somewhat similar" to their fathers'. Those data reflect 78% and 72% respectively. Religious similarity to parents varies by the religious tradition the teens belong to, as do many of the other religious variables found in this study. Here, Mormon teens were the most likely among all U.S. teens to hold religious beliefs like their parents', followed by conservative Protestant, mainline Protestant, Catholic, and black Protestant teens. Jewish teens were the least likely to say they share the same beliefs of their parents', even though this percentage is still an impressive majority. Christian Smith, *Soul Searching*, 35.

13. Merton P. Strommen, Richard A. Hardel, *Passing on the Faith: A Radical New Model for Youth and Family Ministry* (Winona, MN: Saint Marys Press, 2000), 98.

14. John Losey, *Experiential Youth Ministry Handbook: How Intentional Activity Can Make the Spiritual Stuff Stick* (El Cajon, CA: Youth Specialties, 2004), 23.

15. Perry Downs, *Teaching for Spiritual Growth: An Introduction to Christian Education* (Grand Rapids, MI: Zondervans, 1994), 200.

16. Merton P. Strommen, Richard Hardel, *Passing on the Faith*, 159.

17. What appears here is a summary of the Valuegenesis research by the Seventh-day Adventist church in its 1990 and 2000 survey results on faith, values and commitment found in V. Bailey Gillespie, Michael Donahue, *Ten Years Later: A Study of Two Generations*, 223-225.

18. Sharon Daloz Parks, *Big Questions, Worthy Dreams* (New York, NY: Jossey-Bass, 127

chapter 10

understanding the implications

In my university class with the title of Religious Faith and Life, I begin a discussion about personal faith by spending time exploring religious experience together. In general terms, personal religious experience is best explained using a three-point model. (1) *Content*; (2) *Feelings*; (3) *Response*.

Now I know that this is simplification of a complex personal and religious phenomenon, but after exploring a number of models suggested by both theologians and psychologists of religion, I try to boil their complex models down to something that students will remember.

This three-part model allows me to explore the facts *(content)* of one's religious experience, evaluate the emotions *(feelings)* that we all experience as we draw closer to God, and the logical results *(response)* that come through responsibility to the life-changing content of faith. And I begin this discussion by using the Book of Romans in the New Testament to explore the way the Apostle Paul understands his own content, feelings, and response in faith. I believe when you arrive at the 8th chapter of this wonderful book, you can see the centrality of Christ, the beauty of grace, the importance of following the "way." Paul develops all this in only seven chapters.

It seems important to me to dry to boil down this deep discussion of faith into these three elemental categories for one simple reason. *I want my students to remember how their religious life is configured, what they believe, how they feel about that belief, and how that configuration plays out in their everyday lives.*

Some may think this is simplistic, but I have seen over the years students make serious commitments to God because they finally understand their own religious life and growth seen in that model. And since I have them journal their experience during the quarter, I get a chance to watch their lives change as they reflect on the content of their faith according to the Apostle Paul in the New Testament.

It is no different when we review the principles laid down in this book, *Hey! Love Them and They Will Come.* This must be the first understanding by both youth and young adult religious educators in the local church and among the teachers in Christian education. So it seems natural to review some basic understandings that we have explored. And we also recognize that repetition is good for the soul as well as a wonderful learning tool.

What conclusions can we draw in light of our conversation about youth and young adults and their involvement in the church?

Try as we might to understand the reasons youth and young adults fail to become attached to the church, this may actually be a futile exercise. Face it, there are a lot of reasons not to get involved in anything, much less the church.

But what we do know for sure is that like people, churches often exhibit personality traits that characterize their central foci and purpose. I believe it is these traits that often drive the young from active commitment and deepening involvement with their local congregation. And we can name a few traits that just stand out and become an identity tag for all to see.

churches that place belief above relationships.

Now, just wait; I did not say beliefs are unimportant. We have already made the case that what we believe provides a framework for understanding commitment, and our beliefs shape the way we view God and how He works in this world. After all, if we did not have a doctrine of salvation, we would never know the reasons for faithfulness, never know what the Bible says about it, and never understand the logic of the love of God for this world. But church concern that places belief before relationships is a personality trait often experienced by the young as a church that is more interested in truth for truth's sake, than the way that truth changes our lives. It seems to some that people would rather be right than loving!

This personality trait comes across to the young as cold, calculating, absent from love, and all too often judgmental as the young are trying to establish their own personal theological identities.

We wish that everyone would know what they believe, and how the Bible explores that truth, and why that truth is important to their actual living life in the world. So truth must always be presented with the reasons why it is important. After all, Christ is truth; therefore, He must be in all truth too. Ask yourself where your church places understanding doctrinal truth in light of the growing, simple need for young people of feel God's love and acceptance before—yes, before they establish the truth for themselves. Learning always is best when you understand the reason to learn. It is the same way with Truth. Knowing Christ and His love precedes knowing what that love implies in our life, our mind, and in our relationship with others in the world.

yes, it just may be the their fault!

Well, not completely, but if that phrase catches your attention, then we've done our job! Parents make a lot of difference. Yes, the church has responsibility too, but first and foremost good parenting, open, loving, compassionate, with clear boundaries evidenced through conversations and personal witness to the power of God in their lives makes a huge difference when it comes to understanding the church and providing a welcoming climate for young people..

We have heard over the years the fact that young people often get their only picture of God through the eyes and actions of their parents. If this is true as many share, then helping Christians parent must be a priority in the church. We believe no thriving youth and young adult ministry forgets that parents need nurture, education, and understanding too.

When was the last time your church ran a parenting program

for your membership? Have you ever seen a church with a grand-parenting program outlined to help them understand their young grandchildren? Have you ever seen more than one sermon a year talk directly to parents about their skills and the fact that they are the major picture of God and the church that their own children may see? Parents are very central to any good youth and young adult program, so don't forget to spend time helping them understand their youth, as well as understand the Gospel.

try this. *Parenting Skills for Kids.* Invite parents and youth to an afternoon meeting, then separate both groups. You will need two leaders to do this right. Then ask these questions. "If you could tell your parents anything about good parenting, what would you say?" Do the same for the adults, only ask, "If you could tell your children about being good kids, what would you say?" Do the same about what they think the church is like—have both groups provide descriptive words that share their understanding of church. Then send a "missionary" from each group to share each group's conclusions. Finally, bring the groups back together for a wrap-up and debriefing. Then have some food and fellowship before closing the seminar with prayers by members of both groups.

can you guarantee balance?

We want to remind you again about the importance of being true to your mission and letting the message, activities, and purpose flow directly from a clearly designed and owned mission. When contemporary churches talk about being a missional church, they simply mean a church that is acting out of a commitment to be compassionate. Compassion for others might be your mission too. Understanding God's love might be your mission focus. Committing our lives to Jesus as the ONE, might be it too. Or, perhaps, learning about our church could be the mission you have derived from conversations with your church and young people. But try to identify early on in your group just what your foci will be.

After mission come the elements of ministry that explore, clarify, or otherwise demonstrate the mission in action. Here such things as Bible study, evangelism, understanding prayer, exploring compassion could all be elements that your ministry at your church identifies in order to fulfil your mission. Whatever your elements are, they should bring balance to your ministry.

People often ask us how many elements should be in a ministry? This is a personal decision, brought about through conversations with the youth, pastoral staff, elders, parents, and of course, your youth and young adults. Once clarified, these elements help share a maturity of faith and belief and frame the focus of your programming, concerns, insights, and study. In reality, you can only do three or four in one year clearly enough for all of the youth to grasp their personal meaning. So don't clutter your ministry with too many target issues or goals. Remember, you are with your young people on a journey, and there are lots of detours and stops on the way. "Too much too soon" should be your caution, and always remember to make Jesus the very central motivational force in your targets in ministry.

thinking builds maturity; warmth creates community

We talked as well about the central role that these two kinds of climates have in helping young people to become attached to their local congregations or group. The sense of warmth, welcoming, belonging, usefulness, and ownership build a mature faith, while at the same time developing openness, critical thinking skills, and acceptance of new ideas builds loyalty as well. Sensing a church as warm and being proud of your church for its critical thinking skills results in positive attitudes toward the church. It may not eliminate all of the reasons why your young people leave the church, but having them experience this in the church will go a long way towards inviting them to remain.

It is not uncommon to hear young people question their beliefs and express a desire to be stretched to think about difficult things. Of course, the older the youth are, the more likely these attitudes are related to their feelings about an authoritative church. But if your church can think clearly about its personality and the message it sends to the young who are struggling with personal identity issues, personal feelings of acceptance and belonging, and start to build a theological identity and belief system that is their own and not their parents', you can see why these two characteristics, if found in their home church, will keep them coming back for instruction, guidance, and community.

making jesus the very center

We have been trying to explore the ways that young people attach themselves to the local church and at the same time understand the reasons that they all too often disappear after they move away from home or get out on their own. And as you can see, there are no easy answers, although some things have become clear. In concluding this chapter, it seems very important to talk one more time about the focus of religion itself in one's life.

There is only one pure motivation for individuals to become close to a local congregation that is living the message of God through their mission, outreach, lifestyle, personality, and focus. After all, why would anyone want to spend an eternity someplace where friends didn't even know your name, relationships were broken, and attitudes were unacceptable. And the reason that this is so clear is because the young in the church often go "missing" even while they are attending regularly.

Perhaps it is because they don't see in the church a motivation that is better than the things that distract them in this world. They see their friends fighting, judging them, arguing over territory and turf. They see their so-called friends backbite others, gossip, share partial truths and stories that are not even close to reality.

The church has a higher model than this, and if young people don't see it, they often are gone, absent in mind and purpose even though they are present in body.

So then, who is the center of the church? Jesus Christ. Gone are the days when your young adults attend your religious community because they are "supposed to." Scott McConnell, associate director of LifeWay Research, says that "Only 10% of those who continued attending church did so to please others. Young adults whose faith truly became integrated into their lives as teens are much more likely to stay in church. If church did not prove its value during their teen years, young adults won't want to attend—and won't attend."[1]

Teacher, apologist and author Voddie Baucham explains it best when he says, "Going to church doesn't make one a follower of Christ anymore than standing in a garage makes one a car."[2] But in reality, going to church regularly and learning to live with the church—the body of Christ— are desires that naturally come from a person's heart that has been changed by love for the Gospel of Jesus.

jesus is the one, period, full stop

A long time ago, 1991 to be exact[3], there was a movie with Jack Palance and Billy Crystal. There were others in the movie as well, but who can remember them? They were just peripheral to the theme of the movie. And while the movie was about a city kind of guy out in the wilderness, there was one pivotal scene. The scene had Jack Palance's character explaining to Billy Crystal that there was only "one" thing worth living for. In fact, there was only one thing worth dying for! That thing was never explained to us, it was left to our own understanding of what is important to each person. However, we see things a bit differently.

As Christians, we have a much better idea of what that "one" thing truly is. Jesus Himself claims to be this "One" thing in John 14:6: *"Jesus answered, "I am the way and the truth and the life. No one comes to the Father except through me."*

This Jesus we are to believe in actually transcends the way that we talk of Him. If He is the way, the TRUTH, and the life, then we need to spend some time dwelling in Him, rather than simply talking about Him. It is possible that we have spent the majority of our time making sure we have the right belief, but not believing in the right way. This is a big deal. To acknowledge Jesus as all and in all is different than talking about Him. It is a deep sense of abiding, of dwelling, and of living in Him and with Him. He is the ONE thing that binds us, the one thing that unites us, and the one thing that is inter/cross generational, cross-cultural, and defies any boundaries that we might have to put in His way.

If Jesus is all in our experience, then He must be all in our beliefs as well. Here is a great quote from Ellen G. White, an important religious figure of the 19th century, that shares the centrality of Jesus. *"There is one great central truth to be kept ever before the mind in the searching of the Scriptures—Christ and Him crucified. Every other truth is invested with influence and power corresponding to its relation to this theme."*[4]

So to speak of any belief, fundamental or otherwise, and not see how Jesus is essential to the conversation is to simply miss the point. Jesus is the milk and the meat of our faith. Jesus is not something that we get past in order to deal with the weightier issues of doctrine; He is the impetus that gives the doctrines their heft, girth and length. They are not weighty without Jesus in the midst of them. The work of a Christian is always, first and foremost, to expose Christ to the world in all we say, see and do. We are Jesus people first, and that is the elemental value that we must transfer to young people in the church.

But, you may think, what of our culture, our own particular beliefs and expressions of faith? How is Jesus expressed in every aspect of our faith tradition? How can haystacks at a potluck show us the love and personhood of Jesus?

look at yourself

To answer this, you only have to look in the mirror. If you are abiding in Christ, then He is the word on your lips and the overflow of your heart. Sound trite? We would argue that dwelling in Christ is the call of every Christian. Our testimony is testimony to Christ, and nothing else. The power of which we speak is the power of Christ, and of course, not our own. If this is the case, then we should be constantly expressing that power through acts of compassion and mercy and through the word of encouragement and grace that we give to those in our care.

Young people are looking for a God to love; a God that is worth loving. These longings are expressed by the great theologian Augustine when he states the following as he was reflecting on his youth: "My God, how I burned with longing to have wings to carry me back to you . . . although I had no idea what you would do with me!"[5] So many young people feel the same way! So many are searching for something that we have, with good intention, made so intangible so as not to be grasped. Truth as proclamation only grasps a two-dimensional God, but truth as a person is to see God in 3-D. It is a 360-degree, surround-sound God that can no longer be only spoken of, but demands being spoken to.

are your young people ready?

Yes is the answer. Youth and Young Adults are ready for this kind of connection. Kenda Creasy-Dean, in speaking of many of those who throughout Christian history have sought that connection with God states: "In short, they (Bernard of Clairvaux, Catherine of Siena, Martin Luther, Jonathan Edwards) believed that the more we align ourselves with the life and death of Jesus Christ – his Passion – the more we find ourselves integrated into the life of God, and the more readily we reach out to those who suffer."[6]

So as we close this book, we want to challenge you to reorder your priorities, find a new center of your life, and model the Kingdom of God to your young people.

You must earn the right to speak the name of Jesus Christ into the lives of those you influence. His name, His person is the greatest gift of all. We speak of grace only in connection with the grace giver. And we are given grace only by what He did on the cross and His ultimate resurrection and ascension. This is now our gift to give, and we give it with authenticity, in the context of our own faith journey. We invite those around us to walk with us in this faith, and we carry one another when it is needed. We are passionate about this and we believe that this passion, this Christ-centered focus for your ministry will open the way for God to reach your young people and help them make choices to include the local church in their lives as well as to choose Jesus Christ as their own personal God.

The only reason we can do any of these things is because of the power of Jesus Christ on the cross. This Jesus, and particularly our understanding of Him, must go beyond church stories and be seen in 3-D. Gone are the felts that we learned Jesus through, and in their place is the living, breathing son of God, member of the trinity, and fully human lamb of God.

I was in Costco the other day, and they had the 3-D televisions on display. At first I thought, "What a stupid idea. Who would wear glasses to watch TV?" But then I went and took a look. And while I still feel that the glasses portion is a bit of a pain -- it takes a bit of thought and commitment -- the quality of the picture is really quite worth it.

That is the God that we serve. This is the Jesus that is surround-sound, 3-Dimensional TRUTH. We need look no further for the author and definer of our faith. He is the wave that never breaks, the tone that always resonates and the power behind our words. To give this name to future generations is to truly love them and give them a peace that is beyond what we understand. This is the truth of the Gospel, and this is the good news that compels us toward acts of compassion and mercy in His name.

It's simple. Too simple sometimes. But the premise of all that comes before this leads us back to Jesus the Christ. Abide and dwell in Him. And may His grace be to you good news!

Yours now, for excellence in youth and young adult ministry.

chapter 10 / endnotes

1. Scott McConnell in "Church? No thanks. Why teens are leaving in droves." By Rebecca Grace, *AFA Journal*, May 2008, 1 in http://www.onenewsnow. com/Journal/stories.aspx?id=75927.

2. *Ibid.*, 1.

3. Found in http://www.imdb.com/title/tt0101587/.

4. Ellen G. White, MS 31, 1890.

5. Augustine, Confessions, tran. R.S. Pine-Coffin (Harmondsworth, U.K.: Penguin Books, 1961), 59.

6. Kendra Creasy Dean, *Practicing Passion: Youth and the Quest for a Passionate Church*, xi.

extras

extra a

reasons teens avoid church

the research says forget pizza parties

recent research from the Barna Group, a Ventura, California evangelical research company, argues that only about one I four teens now participate in church youth groups and numbers have been flat since 1999 to 2009.

Thom Rainer, president of LifeWay Christian Resources in Nashville, Tennessee, claims that "Sweet 16 is not a sweet spot for churches. It's the age teens typically drop out. . . . A decade ago teens were coming to church youth groups to play, coming for the entertainment, coming for the pizza. They're not seen coming for the pizza anymore. They say, 'We don't see the church as relevant, as meeting our needs or where we need to be today.'"[1]

But are teens and young adults any busier than their peers were decades ago? Sure, they spend Time on Facebook and Twitter their friends. Shane Raynor, blogger on the Faith Experience website, identifies five reasons why teens are avoiding church:[2]

1. *"Teens don't show up because they don't think God is showing up."* He suggests unique insights into this dilemma. "If the power of God isn't moving in your church's youth group beyond the free pizza and the basketball,. . . . you're eventually going to hit a wall. This is where churches really mess up, . . .Gimmicks are like the dot come bubble of the late 90s. Sooner or later, everyone wants substance, and if it isn't there, they're going to bail."

2. *"Teens don't make church a priority because their parents don't make it a priority."* This reflects the centrality of spiritually minded and practicing parents. Good parents make good kids, so the saying goes. Young people take their cues from their folks, and often church is not a regular priority for the parents. And since young teens don't drive to church themselves, parents have to have a certain degree of commitment in order to make church happen. Raynor continues, "Man up and be your kid's parent, not their friend. But before you do that, you might want to make sure you're participating in worship and Bible study yourself. You'll stand a better chance of avoiding the whole hypocrisy factor."[3]

3. *"Teens are very connected to each other now and don't need church to hook up anymore."* The Christian church has a fundamental bias about relationships. Church is a place where you come to meet and fellowship with your friends. Well, that was true; not so much now. Social networking has eliminated church as a necessary gathering place. You can hang out at home, close to your computer or smart phone, and then you don't have to sit through a message just to see your friends. Raynor says to this argument, "sad, but true."

4. *"Unchurched teens see no significant difference between church kids and everyone else."* As a professor of theology and Christian personality I hear this phrase more times than I would like. Are the young people in church much different than every other teenager? The answer is yes and no. But as Raynor says, "Suppose you were thinking about joining a diet program where the participants never lost any weight? Or a gym where no one ever showed any physical progress? Or a karate school where no one ever got a black belt? You'd see it as a waste of time."[4] Young people are not looking for perfection, but they would like to see some progress in how religion makes a difference in the members' lives. So take church seriously, move the people to change and grow with Christ as the very center of their motivation and see if the young in the church take notice.

5. *"Many teens get impatient with churches that major on the minors and try too hard to seem relevant."* Over the years I have seen one common complaint about church from many teens and

young adults: an over-emphasis on behavior and life style choice. Of course, youth and young adult professionals, adult leaders, and, of course, parents often are concerned about the choices that their young people make and this concern can be perceived as judgmental. Young people who are the target of such discussions feel that they can never be good enough.

This perception as negative is part of the climate issues in many churches. Merton P. Strommen and Richard Hardel share some observations that are appropriate in their book, *Passing on the Faith, A Radical Model for Youth ad Family Ministry* as they describe two types of church members, based on the qualities forming each family: Gospel-oriented church members and law-oriented members:

gospel-oriented members.
() Value a spiritual dimension to life
() Know a personal, caring God
() Are relatively certain of their faith
() Consider their faith to be important
() Take a positive attitude toward life and death and reject the idea of a salvation by works alone

law-oriented members
() Cannot tolerate change
() Have a need for religious absolutism
() Tend to be prejudiced
() Feel threatened by those different from themselves
() believe in a salvation by works. They believe they gain favor with God by what they do.[5]

Couple climate control actions with an emphasis on Jesus Christ and His grace and love, and young people will feel wanted, will feel their membership in the religious community is important, and their identity formation will include Jesus as the ONE who provides the motive for change. A grace orientation implies more than simply believing in the bountiful love of God towards us, it motivates us to be the kinds of people God expects, died for, and will soon come again to receive.

research insights. There is ample research that explores the reasons why young people are avoiding or leaving the church. Here is a summary of some of the most interesting studies on this topic.

() The survey by the American Research Group of 1,000 20-29-year olds who used to attend evangelical churches on a regular basis found a "Sunday School Syndrome," indicating children who faithfully attend Bible classes in their church over the years actually are more likely to question the authority of Scripture. Among the survey findings, regular participants in Sunday School are more likely to: (1.) Leave the church; (2.) Believe that the Bible is less true; (3.) Defend the legality of abortion and same-sex marriage; and (4.) Defend premarital sex. This is a clear call for reevaluation and revision in our religious education program in the church.[6]

() *Christianity Today* identifies some cultural trends that are important to understand. Drew Dyck in his blog identifies 'mile markers" that show up in the lives of young adulthood: "leaving for college, getting the first job and apartment, starting a career, getting married—and for many people today, walking away from the Christian faith."[7] He quotes a 2009 study from the American Religious Identification Survey (ARIS) claiming the percentages of Americans who select "no religion" almost doubled in the last two decades, moving form a low of 8 percent in 1990 to 15 percent in 2008. And some 22 percent of the 18-29-year-olds claimed no religion, which was up from 11 percent in 1990. The study also shared that "73 percent of the 'Nones' (no religious affiliation) came from religious homes; 66 percent were described by the study as 'de-converts.'"[8]

() The Pew Forum on Religion and Public Life presented research from their book *American Grace,* released in 2010. They reported that "young Americans are dropping out of religion at an alarming rate of five to six times the historic rate 930-40 percent have no religion today, versus 5-10 percent a generation ago)."[9]

() In his book, *Unchristian*, David Kinnaman, president of the Barna Research Group, relayed his findings from thousands of interviews with young adults. His findings include the following, "The vast majority of outsiders [to the Christian faith] in this country, particularly among young generations, are actually dechurched individuals."[10]

() Ken Ham and Britt Beemer in their book, *Already Gone*, explore reasons why young adult evangelical Christians leave the church. The ten top reasons are:

#1 — 12% say the services are boring
#2 — 12% claim legalism in the church
#3 — 11% identify hypocrisy of church leaders
#4 — 10% think the church is too political
#5 — 9% cite self-righteous people
#6 — 7% feel church is too distant from their home
#7 — 6% regard as not relevant to personal growth
#8 — 6% God would not condemn to hell
#9 — 5% Bible not relevant and not practical
#10 — 5% couldn't find my preferred denomination nearby[11]

how should you respond?

As you can see, the reasons that 25-30-somethings leave the church are complex. If we try to identify the exact reasons we probably would have to write another book. What might we conclude about this topic?

1. *A significant part of leaving the church has to do with the new culture we are in.* We can't do much about changing that; however, in the church we have control of how we respond to the culture.

2. *Responses can be both positive or negative regarding their leaving.* For example, we often have at least two reactions when we hear that someone has left the church. First a negative response. Some might become defensive and try to judge the person who has left, attributing his or her movement away from the church as caused by wrong doctrines, bad judgement, or negative choices. Research shares that almost all who left claimed that "before they left the faith, they were regularly shut down when they expressed doubts. Some were ridiculed in front of peers for asking 'insolent questions.' Others reported receiving trite answers to vexing questions and being scolded for not accepting them. One was slapped across the face, literally."[12] Second, the response could be more positive, but seldom is it seems. Remember, positive reinforcement is the best motivation for change. Religious leaders could learn much from this maxim.

3. *People come back to the faith when the church undertakes the slow*

but fruitful work of building close, deep relationships with those that have left them. "Doubt may not be anything more than 'the tortured language of spiritual longing.'"[13]

We have already mentioned that one of the first jobs of the congregation that sees retaining young people in the church as their priority is to build real relationships with them. "Love them and they will come" is a truism that simply can't be denied or ignored. Building close personal and long-term relationships with the young in the church may stem the tide of departure and alienation. After all, if you feel you are known, people not only recognize you, you feel like you belong. If you are absent from the congregation the members should let the young person know they truly miss them. It is hard to be separated from your friends. And really now, how can you defend a Christ-centered church or ministry that does not have personal compassion at its very core.

how bad are the stats?

Findings from other studies reveal that 97 percent of dropouts from church give specific life-change issues as their core rational for departure. A slim 20 percent predetermined their after high school departure. The most frequent reason for leaving church is, in fact, a self-imposed change, others say, 'I simply wanted a break from church' (27 percent,)' In addition some 25 to 23 percent identified moving to college and work responsibilities prevented them from attending.

As mentioned earlier, the Seventh-day Adventist denominational research completed by Roger Dudley shares that about 48% of high school seniors are disconnected with the church after ten years. This is comparable with other research such as the Assemblies of God studies sharing a 66 percent loss of their students after one year of high school graduation and as much as 82 percent loss of youth after one year of high school in the Southern Baptist denomination.[14]

We all wish these percentages were not as high, however, what is more important than the numbers are the individual young people in your church that might make up these statistics later in life. Living a life of faith comes from a personal motivation to follow Jesus as Lord—Lord of life, Lord of everything, Lord of my life..

Understanding one's relationship with God clarifies things and keeps ou tied to a community tht feels and acts the same way.

The prompting of the Holy Spirit moves for personal decision. When these same young people were children they needed clear loving guidance, but as budding adults they need to understand the importance of personal decision. After all, Jesus again can be our model. Parents and ministry leaders need to let young people make their own decisions based on what has been taught and what is modeled for them. Perhaps Michelle Vu, a Christian Post reporter says it best. "Often what is found is the break from their faith came in the context of relationships, something went wrong with either a youth pastor, a parent, or some other spiritual authority. If they are going to be reconciled, come back to the church, it is going to have to happen in the context of relationships."[15] Love them and they will come. You might just be surprised at how this attitude changes relationships in your church with your youth and young adults.

extra a / endnotes

1. "USA Today, Updated on 8/11/2010. http://www.usatoday.com/news/religion/2010-08-11-teenchurch10_ST_N.htm.
2. Shane Raynor, "5 Reasons Teens are Avoiding Church." http://www.faithexperience.com/2010/08/5reasons/.
3. Rebecca Grace, *AFA Journal*, May, 2008. http://www.onenewsnow.com/Journa/stories.aspx?id=75927.
4. Shane Raynor, "5 Reasons Teens are Avoiding Church." 2-3.
5. *Ibid.*, 3.
6. *World Net Daily*, Wednesday, January 26, 2011. http://www.worldnetdaily.comindex.ph?pageId=100324.
7. *World Net Daily*, June 14, 2009. http://www.wnd.com/index.php?fa=PAGE.printable&pageId=100324.
8. Drew Dyck, *Christianity Today Magazine* on-line posted 11/19/2010, http://www.christianitytoday.com/ct/2010/november/27.40.html?start=5.
9. See Robert D. Putnam and David E. Campbell, *American Grace: How Religion Divides and Unites Us* (New York, NY: Simon & Schuster, 2010).
10. See David Kinnaman, unchristian (Grand Rapids, MI: Baker Books, 2007).
11. Drew Dyck, *Christianity Today Magazine.* 2.
12. *Ibid.*, 3.
13. *Ibid.*, 5.
14. Rebecca Grace, *AFA Journal*, May 2008, 1.
15. Michelle A. Vu, "Generation Ex-Christian Uncovers Why People Leave the Faith," *The Christian Post*, Monday, January 10, 2010. http://cpbooks.christianpost.com/newsrelease/Generation-Ex-Christian-Uncovers-Why-People-Leave-the-Faith/215

extra b

spiritual gift
discovery quiz

instructions: Circle the number you find to be descriptive of your experience: MUCH (3); SOME (2); LITTLE (1); or NONE (0).

M S L N   **descriptions of spiritual gifts**

3 2 1 0   *(1) I enjoy studying the Bible and Sabbath/Sunday school lessons and sharing the insights that God has given me with others.*

3 2 1 0   *(2) When I know that someone is depressed or discouraged I make it a point to contact that person and to cheer him/her up.*

3 2 1 0   *(3) When I speak about a church idea people want to become involved with the idea that I present.*

3 2 1 0   *(4) I have a deep desire to help, through some tangible means, those whom I see are hurting physically, mentally, or spiritually.*

3 2 1 0   *(5) I am able to remain objective and, through the Holy Spirit, find creative solutions for problems that others usually are not even aware of.*

3 2 1 0   *(6) I have faith, even in seemingly impossible situations that everything is going to turn out just fine.*

3 2 1 0   *(7) I would enjoy helping the teacher (who works with children) so that he/she is able to perform his/her task better.*

(8) I enjoy making plans and seeing them carried out.

3 2 1 0   *(9) God has used me to speak to groups of people who don't*
3 2 1 0   *know Jesus, and I have seen many of them give their lives to Him.*

(10) I have a real burden to work with people—to assume the
3 2 1 0   *responsibility in the local church of overseeing others' relationship with God.*

3 2 1 0 *(11) I have taught before, and I believe I am effective.*

3 2 1 0 *(12) When I see someone who looks discouraged, I give a word of encouragement to cheer him or her up.*

3 2 1 0 *(13) I have been told by others that I have the ability to give support and organize action from others for the ideas I present.*

3 2 1 0 *(14) I like bringing flowers or gifts to cheer up someone whom I see is experiencing physical, emotional, or spiritual suffering.*

3 2 1 0 *(15) I have been told by others that God has given me the special ability to solve problems.*

3 2 1 0 *(16) I talk faith continually, even with when I'm discouraged.*

3 2 1 0 *(17) I have the desire to help Christian leaders in our church so they can really get on with their own work.*

3 2 1 0 *(18) I have been told by others that I have the ability to organize.*

3 2 1 0 *(19) I have a compelling desire to stand up before people wh don't know Jesus and talk to them about His grace.*

3 2 1 0 *(20) I find personal enjoyment in working with people very closely and sharing in their joys and sorrows.*

3 2 1 0 *(21) I find it enjoyable to teach people the Bible.*

3 2 1 0 *(22) People often tell me that I have helped make them happier.*

3 2 1 0 *(23) I enjoy leading out and taking charge.*

3 2 1 0 *(24) I would give a book to someone if I thought it would help them to relieve their physical, mental, or spiritual suffering.*

3 2 1 0 *(25) People frequently ask me for counsel.*

3 2 1 0 *(26) I am not easily overcome by difficult situations.*

3 2 1 0 *(27) I would enjoy making the church leaders' work easier.*

3 2 1 0 *(28) I enjoy outlining the necessary steps so that a program or idea can be carried out.*

3 2 1 0 *(29) I would feel comfortable speaking before a group of non-Christians about Jesus.*

3 2 1 0 *(30) I would deeply enjoy working with all kinds of people*

Now simply total up your scores for each gift of the Spirit. The questions that give you the scores are listed in the parentheses on the next page. The Bible texts provide scriptural reference points for discussion of each gift you discover in your own group of spiritual gifts.

_____ A.

_____ B.

_____ C.

_____ D.

_____ E.

_____ F.

_____ G.

_____ H.

_____ I.

_____ J.

A. *Teaching.* A person is able to take concepts from the Word of God and communicate them effectively. Ephesians 4:11-14. (Questions 1,11,21).

B. *Encouraging.* A member is able, through words, to bring comfort, hope, and inner healing. 1 Timothy 4:13. (Questions 2,12, 22).

C. *Leadership.* A member is able to catch a vision of something that needs to be done in the church and others are happy to work with this gifted person in carrying it out. 1 Timothy 5:17. (Questions 3,13, 23).

D. *Mercy.* The unique ability to empathize with people and to alleviate their problems, whether they are spiritual, mental, or physical, thought good works that reflect the love of Christ. Mark 9:41. (Questions 4, 14 24).

E. *Wisdom.* A person who has this gift received special insight on how to apply knowledge to the solving of problems. 1 Corinthians 2:1-13. (Questions 5, 15, 25).

F. *Faith.* This realm of faith is a special gift and differs from faith in general. The person with this gift is able to push forward even in the face of the worst storms of life. Romans 4:18-21. (Questions 6, 16, 26).

G. *Helps.* This gift, with its strange name is seen by those who are able to take their gift to help emphasize the gifts of another person. In this way, the second person can become more effective in his or her work for God. 1 Corinthians 12:28. (Questions 7, 17, 27).

H. *Administration.* A person is able to put plans together that meet the goals of a particular church to help grow the work of God. Acts 6:1-7. (Questions 8, 18, 28).

I. *Evangelism.* The gift of an evangelist is the particular ability to desire to reach people who are non-Christian and to bring them to Jesus Christ. Ephesians 5:11-14. (Questions 9, 19, 29).

J. *Pastoring.* the person who has this gift takes on the responsibility of caring, and strengthening the body of Christ (church membership) in a local congregation. Ephesians 4:11-14, 1 Timothy 3:1-7. (Questions 10, 20, 30).

And finally, from the results of the *Spiritual Gift Discovery Quiz*, enter your three highest gifts in the "dominant" section below. Then enter your next three highest gifts in the "subordinate" section. This will give you an idea of some of the Gifts you have that can be used in your response to God.

Dominant:

      A. _____

      B. _____

      C. _____

Subordinate

      A. _____

      B. _____

      C. _____

In light of the spiritual gifts God has given you, what do you and your pastor, or head elder, youth leader, or teacher see as specific roles that you can fulfill in your local church life?

extra c

bible beliefs survey

try this. *Bible Beliefs Survey.*[8] Give this quick survey to your young people about what they believe. They can select answers from "I have never heard of this" to "I definitely believe this." See how well your youth do with these doctrinal questions. (Feel free to modify these questions to reflect your denominational viewpoint.)

1. God created the world in six 24-hour days
   - ○ I definitely disagree
   - ○ I tend to disagree
   - ○ I'm not sure
   - ○ I tend to agree
   - ○ I definitely agree

2. Jesus will come back to earth again and take the righteous to heaven
   - ○ I definitely disagree
   - ○ I tend to disagree
   - ○ I'm not sure
   - ○ I tend to agree
   - ○ I definitely agree

3. The Ten Commandments still apply to us today
   - ○ I definitely disagree
   - ○ I tend to disagree
   - ○ I'm not sure
   - ○ I tend to agree
   - ○ I definitely agree

4. The true Sabbath is the seventh day—Saturday
   - ○ I definitely disagree
   - ○ I tend to disagree
   - ○ I'm not sure
   - ○ I tend to agree
   - ○ I definitely agree

5. When people die, they remain in the grave until the resurrection
   - ○ I definitely disagree
   - ○ I tend to disagree
   - ○ I'm not sure
   - ○ I tend to agree
   - ○ I definitely agree

5. The wicked will not burn forever, but will be totally destroyed
   - ○ I definitely disagree
   - ○ I tend to disagree
   - ○ I'm not sure
   - ○ I tend to agree
   - ○ I definitely agree

6. The body is a temple of God and we are responsible for its care
   - ○ I definitely disagree
   - ○ I tend to disagree
   - ○ I'm not sure
   - ○ I tend to agree
   - ○ I definitely agree

7. I know that to be saved I have to live by God's rules
   - ○ I definitely disagree
   - ○ I tend to disagree
   - ○ I'm not sure
   - ○ I tend to agree
   - ○ I definitely agree

8. The way to be accepted by God is to try sincerely to live a good life
   - ○ I definitely disagree
   - ○ I tend to disagree
   - ○ I'm not sure
   - ○ I tend to agree
   - ○ I definitely agree

9. I am loved by God even when I sin
   - ○ I definitely disagree
   - ○ I tend to disagree
   - ○ I'm not sure
   - ○ I tend to agree
   - ○ I definitely agree

10. I am worried abut not being ready for Christ's return
   - ○ I definitely disagree
   - ○ I tend to disagree
   - ○ I'm not sure
   - ○ I tend to agree
   - ○ I definitely agree

notes and things to remember